Praise for Ngũgĩ wa Thiong'o's

In the House of the Interpreter

"More than sixty years later, Ngũgĩ continues to wrestle with the greater significance of each event in his formative years, searching for resolution but often only discovering more questions. . . . A useful firsthand look at . . . circumstances, which have played out, and continue to play out, on countless stages around the world."
                                                    —*The Boston Globe*

"Richly moving. . . . [Ngũgĩ's] reconstruction of the era is lucid, the incidents he records from these years are vividly recorded; it's very easy to see the young man slowly changing directions as he becomes one of Africa's great writers and thinkers."   —*CounterPunch*

"Strong and memorable. . . . Ngũgĩ has a remarkable lightness of touch. . . . A document of a remarkable writer's political coming-of-age."   —*The Independent* (London)

"Luckily there was such a sharp mind present at this time and place to record with such perspicacity the confluence of race, politics, war, and literature."
                                                    —*The Daily Beast*

"Amazing. . . . The author easily keeps the balance between the whimsical, political, spiritual and personal."
—*Ebony*

"A particularly powerful indictment of British colonialism and a lasting testament to the healing power of literature. Never bitter or one-sided, tempered throughout by a love of language that cuts across deep cultural divisions, including inter-tribal rivalry. . . . There's much to ponder here."   —*Times Higher Education* (London)

"A fine and fiery book. . . . A compelling memoir."
—*The Scotsman*

"An inspiring story of a young man determined to excel and escape."   —*Kirkus Reviews*

"Alternately youthfully innocent and politically savvy, this is a first-rate telling of that African revolutionary elite who determined the future of their continent."
—*Publishers Weekly*

Ngũgĩ wa Thiong'o

In the House of the Interpreter

Ngũgĩ wa Thiong'o has taught at Nairobi University, Northwestern University, Amherst College, Yale University, and New York University. He is Distinguished Professor of English and Comparative Literature at the University of California, Irvine. His many books include *Wizard of the Crow*, *Dreams in a Time of War*, *Devil on the Cross*, *Decolonising the Mind*, and *Petals of Blood*, for which he was imprisoned by the Kenyan government in 1977.

www.ngugiwathiongo.com

Also by Ngũgĩ wa Thiong'o

In the House of the Interpreter

A MEMOIR

Ngũgĩ wa Thiong'o

Anchor Books
A Division of Random House LLC
New York

The Library of Congress has cataloged the Pantheon edition as follows:
Ngũgĩ wa Thiong'o.
In the house of the interpreter : a memoir / Ngũgĩ wa Thiong'o.
p. cm.
1. Ngũgĩ wa Thiong'o.   2. Authors, Kenyan—20th century—
Biography.   3. Revolutionaries—Kenya—Biography.   I. Title.
PR9381.9.N45Z46 2012   823'.914—dc23 [b]   2012013986

Anchor Books Trade Paperback ISBN: 978-1-101-91051-1
eBook ISBN: 978-0-307-90770-7

Book design by M. Kristen Bearse
Map by Mapping Specialists, Ltd.

www.anchorbooks.com

146028962

TO THE CLASS OF 1958:

George Kinoti
Nicodemus Asinjo
John Wainaina
Elijah Nyanjui
Philip Ochieng
Gerald Macharia
Archie Mbogho
Joshua Omange
David Maringa
Samwel Mwanzia
Joab Onyange
Dunstan Ireri
Joseph Mengo
Meshak Oluoch
John Kang'ethe
John Kimanzi
George Ongute
Ishmael Gatuna

Joel Kori
Nelson Auma
Alexander J. Amega
Archibald Githinji
Andrew Kaingu
James Wafula
Samwel Githegi
David Mzigo
Hiram Karani
Daniel Gatangi
Stephen Muna
Henry Chasia
Erastus Ngunya
James Ngugi*
Kennedy Munavi
Elius Irongo
Samuel Mungai
Peter Bambula

Joseph Gatuiria
Livingstone Nkuruna
Stephen Swai
George Njoroge
Ernest Likimani
Johana Mwalwala
Bethuel Kurutu
Moses S. Kiarie
John G. Mgalu
Erastus Kiaritha
Joseph Njau
Gilbert Kaisha
Julius Kitur
Evanson Mwaniki
Kamau Kiarii
Benjamin Mogaka
James Giceru

A formative part of my intellectual and spiritual strivings

*Ngũgĩ wa Thiong'o

*And in memory of Kenneth Mbũgwa,
who passed on in the middle of my writing this memoir.*

SOMETHING startles me where I thought I was safest.

—WALT WHITMAN,
"This Compost," *Leaves of Grass*

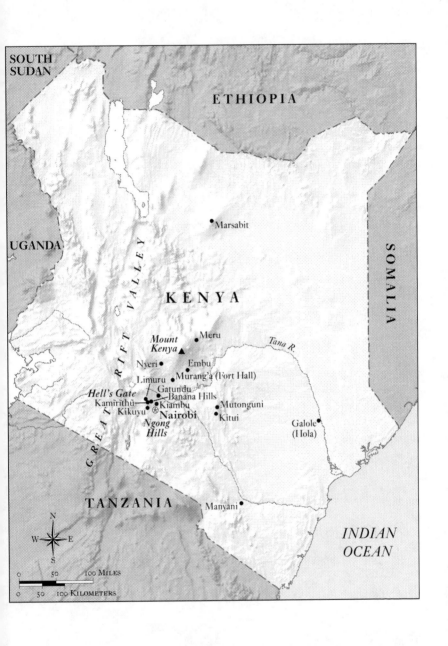

1955

A Tale of Home and School

I

It's the end of my first term at boarding school, and I'm going home. It's April. When I first left Limuru for Alliance High School in January, it was in the last car of a goods train into which I had been smuggled, my sole company then being workmen's tools and clothes. Now I travel third class, with schoolmate Kenneth Wanjai. It's very crowded, standing room only, and our school uniform of khaki shirts, shorts, and blue ties marks us as different from the general passengers, all black Africans, their clothes in different stages of wear and tear. Their haggard faces belie the animated voices and occasional laughter. On getting off at Limuru railway station, I linger on the platform and look around me to savor the moment of my return. The goods shed, the tea kiosk, the waiting room, and the outside toilets marked for Europeans only, Asians only, and Africans, minus the qualifying only, still stand, silent weather-beaten witnesses of time that has passed since the station first opened in 1898.

Wanjai and I part company for our different destinations, he in his father's car, and I alone, on foot. Then it hits me: I'm going home to my mother. Soon, very soon, I'll be with my sisters and younger brother. I have news to share with them: I was among the top of my class. No doubt my mother will ask me if that was the best I could have done, or her variation, were you number one, and I will have to confess that another boy, Henry Chasia, was ahead of me. As long as you tried your best, she will surely tell me with pride. I am going to bask in her sunny smile, which always carries warmth and depth of care. I enjoy her reaction in advance.

I lift my wooden box by the handle with my right hand. It's not very heavy, but it dangles and keeps on hitting against my legs. After a time, I change hands; it's worse on the left side, so I lift it onto my shoulder. I keep up the pattern: right hand, left hand, right shoulder, left shoulder, and back to the right hand. My progress is slow. I walk past the African marketplace, which looks deserted, a ghostly place, except for a pack of stray dogs, chasing and fighting over a female in heat. But the memory of my childhood interactions with the place floods back: my brother's workshop; people massing outside the Green Hotel to hear news; my falling off Patrick Mũrage's bike. I stagger up the slope toward the Indian shopping center. Almost two years back, my brother, Good Wallace, ran down this very slope, barely escaping a hail of police bullets, but I refuse to let memories of pain interfere with my first homecoming as an Alliance student. Instead, I conjure up images from my Limuru youth that are more in tune with my triumphant mood.

Onesmus Kĩhara Warũirũ immediately comes to my mind. Kĩhara, an incredible cyclist and showman to boot, loved climbing this slope. People used to stand aside and cheer him in wonder and admiration as he cycled up the hill to take mail and parcels to the Indian shopping center. No other cyclist had ever managed to climb the hill all the way without once getting off his bike and pushing it. Kĩhara was our bike hero, possessor of superhuman endurance.

I'm so engrossed in these thoughts that I forget to take note of the landscape around me. But instinct suddenly tells me that I have gotten home . . . or where home should be. I stop, put down the box, and look around me. The hedge of ashy leaves that we planted looks the same, but beyond it our homestead is a rubble of burnt dry mud, splinters of wood, and grass. My mother's hut and my brother's house on stilts have been razed to the ground. My home, from where I set out for Alliance only three months ago, is no more. Our pear tree is still standing, but like the ashy hedge, it's a silent witness. Casting my eyes beyond, I suddenly realize the whole village of homesteads has disappeared. The paths that had crisscrossed the landscape, linking the scattered dwellings into a community, now lead from one mound of rubble to another, tombs of what has been. There is not a soul in sight. Even the birds flying above or chirping in the hedges emphasize the emptiness. Bewildered, I sit on my box under the pear tree, as if hoping it will share with me what it knows. The tree, at least, has defied the desolation, and I pick a few ripe pears to eat in baffled silence. How could a whole village, its people, history, everything, vanish, just like that?

The sight of two rats chasing each other amid the rub-

ble shakes me out of my reverie. I think of going toward
the only houses still standing, the Kahahus', despite their
ghostly aura, for an answer. Once again I stagger along with
the box. At the hedge, I see a man and recognize Mwangi,
part of a group of workers who have always rendered loyal
services to the Kahahu family. As children, we called him
Mwangi wa Kahahu, although he was not blood related. He
always had gossip about the goings-on in the big house on
the hill. Now he and I are the only humans in a desolate
landscape.

You mean you don't know that all the people have been
moved to near the home guard post? Oh, but of course you
have come home on school break. Go up, and you will see
for yourself, he says, gesturing vaguely in the direction of
the ridge.

His delivery is matter-of-fact. I stare at him, waiting for
more, but he walks away. Normally he would have taken the
time to tell tales of the Kahahu family, his favorite subject,
but today he does not have the words. Slowly I work my
way up the ridge, past more piles of rubble, charred funeral
pyres of a rural community. From the top of the ridge, now
bereft of all memories, I put the box down and look at the
valley below. A completely new vista of grass-thatched roofs
lies before me.

Away with images of the past, I tell myself. Distractions
will not help. Take your box and walk down the same path
you used to take to school. Go down the slope. Walk across
the dirt road in the valley below, past the permanent pool of
muddy waters. Force feet to move. Yes, move. Move. Move.
Move on. Drag the box along.

I come to the first line of houses. With some men in the mountains and others in prison, women have willed themselves into old and new roles: feed and clothe the kids; fetch water; work in the fields; stretch out your hands for meager wages; and build. Build new houses. Set up new homes. You don't even have time to survey the work of your hands. You need a stranger, like me, to view what you have no time to see. The huts are in different stages of completion. Armed home guards patrol the paths of the new grass village. No respite for you, our mothers and sisters and children.

I ask people, anybody that comes into view, whether they have seen my mother. Some look puzzled and say they don't know who I'm talking about; others shrug their shoulders or simply shake their heads and continue with the task at hand. But some ask me details about my family, the location of their old homestead, and then point to where I might get more information.

The old independent households from different ridges have been gathered into one concentration village, called Kamĩrĩthũ, without regard to the old neighborhoods. Somehow, eventually, I find my family. My mother and my brother's wife are on the rooftop thatching, with my sister handing them bundles of grass from below. My younger brother and some young men I don't know are filling up the walls with mud. A shout of recognition from my younger brother Njinjũ makes the neighbors stop to look. My sister Njoki wipes her hands on her dress and shakes my hand. My mother calls out, *Tuge nĩ woka*, so you have come back, as if she would rather I had stayed away. My younger brother says, *Karibu*. It is less a welcome to the comfort of the family hearth than an invitation to join them in work. I find a corner, take off my Alliance uniform, and change into old clothes, and within a few seconds, I'm all mud. This is not how I had imagined my return.

And Alliance, where I have now lived eighty-nine days longer than I have lived here? What is it to me, now that this village confronts me as a stranger?

2

When I first stepped onto the grounds of Alliance High School on Thursday, January 20, 1955, I felt as if I had narrowly eluded pursuing bloodhounds in what had seemed a never-ending nightmare. Up to that moment, my life had been spent looking nervously over my shoulder. Since the declaration of the state of emergency in 1952, I lived in constant fear of falling victim to the gun-toting British forces that were everywhere, hunting down anticolonial Mau Mau guerrillas, real or imagined. Now I was inside a sanctuary, but the hounds remained outside the gates, crouching, panting, waiting, biding their time.

The stone buildings, so many in one place and all for us, seemed a veritable fortress, quite a change from the mud and grass-thatched huts I had lived in all my life. Our hosts, who I would later learn were prefects, took us on a tour of the grounds, eventually leading us to our different houses and dorms. Even the word *dorm* sounded splendidly safe and cozy. The beds were in two rows facing each other. Between them were drawers whose flat tops served as tables. My luggage, one box, fit under the bed. The dorm reminded me of the ward in King George Hospital, where I was once admitted because of my eyes, except that it smelled not of hospital but of lavender. I had a real bed, my own, for the first time in my life. The following morning I felt like pinching my skin to convince myself that I was awake.

On Friday, my second day, we registered and sorted out tuition at the bursar's office; on Saturday, we were each issued the school uniform of a pair of khaki shorts and shirts, two cotton T-shirts—white for pajamas, red for work—and a blue tie. With more boys continually arriving on the scene, that first weekend passed quickly as in a soft dream, everything swiftly losing its outline in a mist. The howl of the hounds hovered over the horizon, a distant echo.

3

Founded on March 1, 1926, Alliance High School was the result of a short-lived alliance of Protestant missions of the Church of Scotland, the Church Missionary Society, the Methodist Church, and the African Inland Mission.* It was the first secondary school for Africans in the country and the only reminder of the missions' feel-good moment of togetherness. African graduates of the elementary schools now had an alternative to vocational institutes.

The high school followed the recommendations of the

---

* The Church of Scotland Mission was renamed the Presbyterian Church of East Africa in 1946 after a merger with the Gospel Missionary Society. The Anglican CMS became the Church Province of Kenya.

1924 Phelps-Stokes Commission for Education in East Africa, bankrolled by the New York–based Phelps-Stokes Fund and modeled on the nineteenth-century system for educating Native Americans and African Americans in the South. In 1924–25, just before his formal appointment as the first principal of Alliance, G. A. Grieves had gone to America on a Phelps-Stokes grant to study that system, which meant an almost mandatory pilgrimage to Tuskegee and Hampton. Virginia Hampton Institute, founded in 1868 by General Samuel C. Armstrong, the son of a missionary in Hawaii, and Tuskegee Institute in Alabama, founded in 1881 by Booker T. Washington, a graduate of Hampton and protégé of Armstrong, were the models. These schools inspired two almost contradictory educational visions: the notion of self-reliance and the aim of producing civic-minded blacks who would work within the parameters of the existing racial state.* Alliance was set up with this animating spirit. The school motto, Strong to serve, and its anthem, celebrating strength of body, mind, and character, were a rewrite of Armstrong's vision of integrating body, heart, and hands. The theme was repeated in the school's prayer: *Have in thy keeping, O Lord, our God, this school; that its work may be thorough, and its life joyful. That from it may go out, strong in*

---

* Even within America, this system did not always produce the intended results, as shown by the activities of Simbini Mamba Nkomo, founder and executive secretary of the Pan-African Drive by the African Student Union of America, and by the antidiscrimination unrest in African American colleges, including Hampton (1924–27). Kenneth King, *African Students in Negro Colleges: Notes on the Good African* (Phylon, 1960), vol. 31, no. 1970, p. 29.

body, mind, and character, men who in thy name and with thy power will serve their fellows faithfully.

Although Alliance, initially a two-year institution, had literary education at its core, the vocational character of its American South model was maintained through classes in carpentry and agriculture. And like its models, it produced mostly teachers, some later employed in mission and government schools and the independent African schools, before their ban. This model was to remain fairly intact until 1940, when Edward Carey Francis took over as principal and grafted a four-year English grammar onto its vocational American stem.

Carey Francis saw Alliance as a grand opportunity to morally and intellectually mold a future leadership that could navigate among contending extremes, a view he articulated in a letter on April 24, 1944, to Reverend H. M. Grace, Edinburgh House, Eaton Gate:

> Racial feeling in Kenya is bad. There are faults on both sides. Among many Europeans there is suspicion of missions and of education ("spoiling the native") though this is far better than it was; among Africans there is inborn suspicion of the white man. A man who tries to do his job is pretty certain of criticism from both sides, not made easier by the fact that he is bound to make mistakes. But it is a grand opportunity, too. Most of the future leaders of the country pass through our hands.

In another write-up, Carey Francis tells how, on arrival in Mombasa in October 1928, a well-meaning acquaintance

Edward Carey Francis;
taken from *Alliance High School:
75th Anniversary, 1926 to 2001* (110)

from the voyage took him aside and advised him to be careful not to do any work himself, not even straightening out
his mixed-up luggage, for that would mean "losing all pres-
tige with the natives."* Yet the African boys he met at his
first post, as principal at Maseno High School, exhibited a
natural friendliness and innate gentlemanliness, raw material that could be shaped in the right way.

He must have carried that attitude with him to Alliance,
and the school had indeed produced its fair share of an
essentially cooperative leadership. But contrary to the conscious intentions of its founders, Alliance had also birthed

---

* L. B. Greaves, *Carey Francis of Kenya* (London: Rex Collins, 1969), p. 6.

a radical anticolonial nationalist fever. Ironically, in its very structure, Alliance actually subverted the colonial system it was meant to serve, and Carey Francis, an OBE, would turn out to be the most consistently subversive of the colonial order. The presence of Africans on the staff as equals with the white teachers undermined, in our eyes at least, colonial apartheid and the depiction of the African as inferior. Indeed, some of them were more effective in the classroom than their white counterparts. But no matter what or how they taught, the African teachers were role models of what we could become. By insisting on high performance on the playing field and in the classroom, Carey Francis produced self-confident, college-prepared, intellectual minds. By the time I left Alliance, I felt that academically I could go toe to toe with the best that any European or Asian schools could produce.

But when I first arrived, in January 1955, I was not aware of the history behind the school nor of the confidence it would eventually inspire in me. Not that it would have mattered. It was enough for me to know that the hounds could not enter the grounds to disturb my sleep in Dorm Two of Livingstone House.

4

Had I but died an hour before this chance, I had lived a blessed time; for, from this instant, there's nothing serious in mortality. It was about five, on Monday, my fourth morning in Dorm

Two. Why this talk of death? I thought as I sat up, looking apprehensively around me. The morning crier stood in the common yard, outside. The rest of us were in varying degrees of wakefulness. Arap Soi, second year, next to my bed, calmed me down: It's Moses Gathere, the house prefect, his way of welcoming a new day. Or rather, his way of telling the prefects of the four Livingstone dorms to get us moving.

Had I but died, Moses started again. Another boy snorted loudly to nobody in particular, Nincompoop. That's Stanley Njagi, Soi said. He doesn't like to wake up, and he doesn't like being woken up. He covers himself completely with a blanket and reads with a flashlight late into the night. He loves the word *nincompoop.*

By the time Moses was set to crow a third time, like the biblical rooster, everybody had jumped out of their beds, gone out to the bathroom outside, and come back to change from their pajamas into their work clothes, the garments we were given on Saturday. Some boys said they looked like those worn by prisoners, but I didn't mind them. It's clean-up time, Moses was saying again loudly, adding, Cleanliness is second to godliness. This generated laughter that relaxed the morning tension, except in the case of one boy who mimicked the crier: *Had I but a dagger in my hands,* he mumbled, *I would . . .*

And that's Stephen Mũrĩithi, Soi said. He resents authority. He's always combative, as if trying to pick a fight, although he doesn't let it get that far. But his I'm-ready-to-take-you-on stare can be intimidating.

The dorm hived with activity immediately. Without any Shakespearean dramatics, Bethuel A. Kiplagat, the Dorm Two prefect, calmly, efficiently, but authoritatively divided up the morning chores, with the new boys spread out among the veterans: some to clean the dorm; others to cut the grass with scythes and clear the compound; others to clean the toilets and bathrooms outside.

Stories about the toilets were passed on from the older boys, from long ago when they were first introduced. Some students had used the new seating toilets as if they were another version of the old pit latrines, squatting instead of sitting on them and thus often missing the bowl. Nobody would claim responsibility for the resulting mess, and no student volunteered to clean up. Threats of force were met with stony silence. No boy wanted to be thought of as a *chura*, a shit cleaner. Finally, in response, the white teachers took brooms and water and other material and did the work. The resistance was broken. Cleaning toilets became an accepted, normal part of the morning chores.

After cleanup, we came back inside and stood by our beds, while the house master, David Martin, accompanied by Moses Gathere, inspected the dorm, a kind of intrahouse competition among the four Livingstone dorms for tidiness and preparation for the *jembe* inspection.

We then rushed for the showers. I hesitated to remove my clothes in front of the others. In my village, the circumcised and the uncircumcised would never have shared showers, but here that's what everybody, including the prefects, was doing. The school had obviously broken such divisions, for nobody seemed bothered by any other person's nakedness. Some were already soaping themselves, while humming tunes or shouting at one another. Stop staring and get in, somebody yelled at me.

After the showers, we were to get ready for the morning parade, a phrase that conjured up magic. Truly, every day, hour, minute, and second in the school was producing something new and strange, with promises of more to come. I put on my khaki uniform and blue tie with initials AHS and merged into a khaki uniformity, as everyone trooped to the parade ground, which turned out to be the same place we had disembarked on the first day. This fact did not dim the light of its wondrous newness: it may have been an empty *muram* surface, but I would soon learn it was one of the most important spots in the entire school, the site of a daily performance of power.

We stood in lines in the order of our houses, and within each house according to our heights, the tallest in the back. We faced a tall pole with a rope loosely hanging down its side. The senior prefects stood in front of their houses, the house masters a few steps ahead, facing us. The other teachers stood in groups of twos and threes, nonchalant spectators. I had never seen so many white teachers, and my eyes fell on the four black teachers, points of identification.

Suddenly Moses Gathere shouted: Attention. Members of Livingstone responded immediately. Appearing apparently from nowhere, the acting principal, James Stephen Smith, and the school captain, Manasseh Kegode, began their inspection, trailed close behind by the house master and the house prefect. Smith walked along the lines, stopping in front of each boy and examining his clothes, bare feet (shoes were for Saturdays and Sundays only), and hair, deducting points for every instance of discernible untidiness. I thought that I had combed my hair thoroughly, but Smith picked on it and deducted some points from Livingstone. Even in my primary schools, my hair had given me trouble. I had gotten into the habit of pulling my hair or running my fingers through it when absorbed in thought, so no matter how thoroughly I combed it, it looked ruffled after an hour. This was not a good beginning, I told myself.

I was wondering what next, when suddenly I heard sounds of drums, trumpets, and bugles. The band, after a few rounds, stopped by the pole on the raised grass platform in front of us. The entire parade, including the teachers, now stood at attention. Drums purring softly, the drum major walked to the pole in measured steps and attached the folded cloth in his hands to the rope. One of the band boys stepped forward and blew a bugle as the drum major raised the Union Jack. When the flag was finally fluttering in the wind, high up the pole, the assembly sang solemnly:

> God save our gracious Queen,
> Long live our noble Queen,
> God save the Queen!
> Send her victorious,
> Happy and glorious,
> Long to reign over us;
> God save the Queen!

The words and the tune were new to me, but I mumbled along. I don't think I noted the irony in my singing this hymn of prayer while my own brother, Good Wallace, was out in the mountains fighting with the Mau Mau guerrillas so that the queen did not reign long over Kenya.*

After the parade, we trooped to the chapel, a small, steep-gabled building located slightly below one end of the soccer field in a cluster of trees. We took our places in the pews, which held Bibles and hymnbooks, *Songs of Praise* and *Songs of Redemption.* Principal Smith, general inspector of clean bodies, was transformed into a grand inspector of souls. He followed a strict ritual of passages from the Bible and hymns. One hymn caught my attention. Its tone was pleading and fervent, but solemn in its desire: *Wash me, redeemer, and I shall be whiter than snow.*

After chapel, we ran to the dining hall for a breakfast of porridge, unbuttered slices of bread, and cocoa, which we had been asked to bring with us from home. With body and soul fed, we were now ready for what had brought us here from our different places: the diet of the mind.

5

The entire school was divided into two streams, A and B. Before I left home, people in Limuru had talked as if I had done better than any other student in Kenya, a homegrown genius. I was surprised to find, then, that twenty other

---

* I've narrated my brother's dramatic escape into the mountains in my earlier memoir, *Dreams in a Time of War.*

boys had done better than me and were placed in stream A, while I was among the twenty lesser geniuses in stream B. It didn't matter, really: every student learned the same lessons, studied the same texts, and took the same tests. My wings of pride might have been clipped a little, but I was still driven by the pact with my mother: I would always try my best and see what the effort would earn me.

English language was my very first class, and like everything I encountered here, it started with mystery and drama. The potbellied Englishman who entered the class was the same P. R. Oades I had encountered as senior bursar. After introducing himself, he said, Follow me, and walked out. We trooped behind him, across the parade ground, past the soccer field, toward the main gate. He then veered to the left, onto a dirt road that sloped up towards the top of the hill, with gray-stone-walled and brown-tile-roofed bungalows and big manicured lawns on either side. Oades led us to the door of one of these houses: Welcome to my castle. Our first English lesson was a tour of a real Englishman's house.

It started in the living room, the parlor, as we learned, and Oades described its contents: some landscape paintings on the wall, scenes of an English countryside; the carpet, rugs, fireplace, and mantelpiece with candles and china figurines; a cushy sofa set and cushions, side and coffee tables (Not for resting your legs, he hastened to say), a bookcase; and a tall cupboard with plates and glass on display (Not for regular use, he added). In the bathrooms, we discovered bathtubs, sinks, faucets, toothbrushes, and toothpaste.

Everything was in dramatic contrast to my village hut, an all-purpose living space sometimes shared with goats. Our bathrooms were the riversides, where we washed clothes and bathed behind the reeds, and the yard, where we dipped feet or hands in water collected in a basin. In our village, red earth was part of the bathing culture; here, everything was immaculate white.

We moved on to the kitchen, where Oades named the gadgets within: electric cooker, pots, pans, knives (which he described as cutlery), and utensils. In the dining area was a table on which were plates, forks, and knives of various sizes and shapes, and of course, napkins. Oades described how not to sit (Never plant your elbows on the table); how to hold forks and knives, the order of forks and knives, and whether they were used for meat or fish. It was polite to say, Pass the salt please, instead of leaning on another guest to reach out for what one wanted; and of course to tilt the plate away from the body so that one did not spill sauce or soup on oneself. And don't talk with your mouth full of food. There was a lesson on placement of napkins (on the lap, not tucked around your neck), and how to use the tip of a napkin to clear an unwanted something on the lips (but never to blow your nose). We learned that one placed knife and fork crossed or at an angle, preferably a wide angle, to show the waiter that one had not yet finished with the dish at hand, and of course, to place knife and fork together in parallel to tell the waiter that he could now take the plate. We learned about a three-course meal that ended with fruit and dessert. I thought he meant desert, and I wondered how one could eat a piece. Another boy voiced similar doubts. No, it was a dish, not a piece of sand, and the name was *dessert*, not *desert*. We laughed. It was all abstract, so different from my rural cuisine of *ugali* and *irio* that I usually ate with my fingers, certainly without anybody waiting on me. Under the ideals of table manners, Oades was training us into the habit of being waited upon or, at the very least, planting the idea in our minds.

Finally, we moved to the master bedroom, where Oades named mattresses, bedcovers, dressers, drawers, closets, pajamas, and dressing gowns. As he was about to lead us to the guest bedrooms, some of the boys spotted guns hanging on a side porch. Oades wanted to pass on, but the boys stopped, staring. That was a Lancaster machine gun, a Very pistol, and a siren, Oades explained. In 1952, when the Mau Mau War started and the state of emergency was declared, he and David Martin had joined the Kenya Police Reserve. In the early years, they had also armed some students with bows and arrows for night patrol, but the Mau Mau had not yet attacked or even threatened the school. It was clear that Oades was not quite comfortable: guns and their uses were not one of the intended lessons.

As we trooped back to the schoolyard for the next class, we did not discuss this final, jarring note. Instead, we were full of excuse me please, pass the water please, thank you. We recited the order of a three-course meal: starter, soup, main dish, fruit, and dessert, which some still pronounced desert, to a general laughter. Would you like some Sahara? No, no, just a little Kalahari. Most important, some of us chanted, don't hold any food, except fruit, in your hands. This produced more laughter: how would we eat *gĩtheri, irio,* and *ugali* with forks and knives? The *ugali* would lose its taste, someone observed with solemn concern. The pleasures of eating *ugali* lay in touch and taste: dipping fingers into the smoking dish and letting it cool in your mouth, rolling it around with your tongue. He was talking about *English* food, and *English* manners, others added. Overhearing this, Oades explained, before dismissing the class, that table manners had no race or color. Good manners, like cleanliness, were pathways to God and godliness.

6

Oades's subsequent lessons were confined to the classroom, but the English language continued to fascinate me. I discovered that the grammar I had picked up at Kĩnyogori Intermediate School had more than prepared me for high school. Conjugation in general, and the adjectival and adverbial clauses and phrases that made the simple subject-predicate structure into a complex sentence, came easily to me. Literature was an enjoyable extension of my language classes. Ironically, then, it was in a literature class that I first experienced tension with my teachers.

One day Principal Smith, our literature teacher, dwelled on our tendency to use big words to suggest a profound grasp of the language. He read out a sentence from an essay a student had written: As I was perambulating on the road, I countenanced a red-garmented boots-appareled gentleman mounted on a humongous four-legged creature of bovine species. This became the poster sentence for how not to write English.

Avoid words with Latin roots, he told us. Use the Anglo-Saxon word. Above all, learn from the Bible. It has the shortest sentence in English. Jesus wept. Two words. So follow the example of Jesus. He spoke very simple English.

I was puzzled. Not trying to be clever or correct him, I raised my hand and said that Jesus did not speak English: the Bible was a translation. My comment elicited laughter from the class and a sheepish silence from Smith. Then he gave us a short sermon on willingness to learn. Remember you have come here to learn, not to teach. Or do you want to change places with me? he asked, holding out the chalk to me. There was tense silence. He now explained that he was talking about the King James–authorized translation of the Bible, which had inspired many writers of English prose and poetry. It had excellent English, for those who wanted to learn. Smith's testy response froze questions and differing perspectives.

This episode made me recall Kenneth Mbũgua, a fellow student at my primary school, and our frank, often heated debates that left no rancor. In my first few weeks at Alliance, I had looked, in vain, for someone with whom I could argue the way Kenneth and I used to do. I was convinced that Kenneth could have more than held his own with any of my fellow students. It was almost by chance that I was in a high school and he at a teacher-training college, both of us on journeys to different destinations. My performance in English, more than any other subject, had gained me entry into the best of the African secondary schools.

I had not heard from Kenneth since he left for Kambui, and I missed him, especially after my confrontation with Smith. Finally one day I got a large envelope from him. In his letter, he did not tell me tidbits about how he was faring at the teacher-training school, nor ask how I liked Alliance. Instead, he brought up a long-standing argument between us: whether or not one needed a license to write. I'm not sure how I had come to my position, but I had long been adamant that without a license one would risk arrest and imprisonment; Kenneth, on the other hand, was sure that no qualification was necessary. Now he was reviving this heated debate, informing me that he had started writing a book to prove me wrong. He sent me pages as evidence.

His story, about a boy who goes to Nairobi to find work to pay school tuition for himself and his two siblings but gets lost in the corruption of the city, was captivating but too short. Immediately I noted a serious flaw in the telling: he used big words and long sentences. Before, I would have been impressed by the weight of his vocabulary, but now I looked at his work through Smith's eyes. Indeed, Smith's call for us to learn from the example of the English prose in the Bible must have left a mark. The King James–authorized version remained one of my favorite reads. I learned to mix the simple, the compound, and the complex for different effects.

Give me some more pages, I wrote back to Kenneth.

But don't use big words. Read the Bible again and see how English is used. I was about to write that Jesus spoke simple English but caught myself. Still, Smith had given me my first critical tool for evaluating a piece of work.

7

From English literature, history, and geography, we learned new words, titles, facts, and names. From the physics and chemistry labs, it was the vocabulary of beakers, gases, elements, and compounds. H_2O became our new name for water: will you pass some H_2O, please?

I liked physics and chemistry but was often intimidated by the other students, who performed being scientists and talked knowingly with the teachers. I was more intrigued by the magical, alchemistic behavior of elements when mixed or heated together: Why should invisible hydrogen and oxygen make water? for instance. The elements were possessed of spirits. But could I ask my teachers about them?

Biology labs, with their plants in pots and glasses and dead frogs, mice, millipedes, and insects preserved in formaldehyde, smelled of hospitals and death. I gazed at them and imagined them coming back to life and chasing us out of the lab, or simply running away, into the grassy courtyard outside. I grew up surrounded by wild nature. The Manguo marshes were awash with varieties of life: bloodsucking leeches; frogs in their different formations of eggs, legless and legged tadpoles, and young frogs; and birds that laid eggs in the reeds. There was probably a similar variety in the nearby Ondiri marshes. We should have studied them rather than plants isolated in pots or frogs and insects trapped in formaldehyde. Though the labs opened new worlds and made me look differently at the hitherto ordinary, I found the life in books of literary imagination more fascinating than that in history books and scientific laboratories.

8

Allan Ogot, my first math teacher, was tall and exuded confidence and authority. The terms he taught us, *theorem, proof,* and *QED,* became catchwords: statements like *The square of the hypotenuse of a triangle is equal to the sum of the squares of the other two sides,* or *A squared plus B squared equals C squared,* would often crop up in ordinary conversation. They sounded so learned and profound. In his uniform of a scoutmaster, Ogot looked even more imposing and learned. At morning and evening chapel, he gave sermons that were more a soaring challenge to the mind than a roaring call for the soul to fly or hide in shame, surprising us with a more complex English vocabulary than his white counterparts. But it was outside the classroom and the chapel, in a nonteaching setting, that he made the most lasting impression on me. He was not even aware of it. He was standing in the open grass quadrangle, talking to another teacher or a student. He held a book in his hands, and my eyes fell on the title: *Tell Freedom* by Peter Abrahams. I was transfixed.

The words seemed to speak of a world beyond the walls of the Alliance.

Maybe I could have gathered the courage to ask if he could lend me the copy, but I never got around to it, and in August he left for college studies in Scotland. But years later, when I again came across Peter Abrahams and discovered South African literature, I remembered Allan Ogot, standing on the grounds of Alliance High School, silently delivering a sermon through a book title: *Tell Freedom*. That silence was more soaring than any sermon he had given in the chapel and more dazzling than any of the Euclidian theorems.

This would become a pattern in my intellectual growth: passing comments and fleeting images, often outside the formal classroom, would leave a lasting, sometimes pivotal mark on my life.

9

Life was not all mystery and excitement in the sanctuary. One day I was standing alone outside the dining hall when a boy hailed me and stretched out his hand in greeting. When I stretched out mine to grasp his, he quickly withdrew and called out, *Jigger*, who do you think you are? I tried to walk past him, but he blocked my way, calling me *mono*. Finally he let me pass, telling me to mind my manners when speaking to my superiors. It was brutal, humiliating in its total unexpectedness.

In the dining room, I sought out Kenneth Wanjai, a fellow Limurian. Wanjai and I had not known each other well back home, but Alliance had brought us together. He sat beside another student, Leonard Mbũgua, both of them a class ahead of me. They laughed at first, wondering how it was that I had not yet encountered this tradition of harassing freshmen.

They recounted, with relish, stories of newcomers made to wash clothes for their superiors, beaten and driven to sleep in the bush at night, made to give up their entire rations of food, actually burned in front of a fire for refusing to part with their . . . They stopped and laughed, seeing my wide-open eyes. The fire bit was a bit of extra spice, they confessed. That was a long time ago, even before our time, Wanjai reassured me. Besides, I am in Form Two. My friend here and I will protect you.

Their vows of protection did not carry much conviction: they themselves bullied others and were not averse to silencing me with the hated word *mono* when I was winning arguments. I realized that I had to rely on my wits for survival. I seemed to have attracted the evil spirit in the boy who had accosted me. His name, I came to learn, was Benaya Majisu, and I had the bad luck of always encountering him in the most unexpected places. He would ask me to stop, nicely, his palms clasped together as if in prayer, and I would oblige, thinking that he had mellowed, that this time he would apologize. Then he would start opening and closing his palms and would order me to open and shut my mouth to the rhythm of his palm movements. He seemed frustrated when I refused, and I became his challenge. If

Kĩambu students at Alliance High School, 1955:
Kĩmani Nyoike (lying down on right front), Ngũgĩ (second row, third
from left, sitting down), Moses Gathere (first from left, middle row),
Kenneth Wanjai (fourth from left, back row)

a prefect or any other person passed by, he would look like innocence itself. Infuriatingly, I had nowhere to turn for restitution. Who did one complain to that another student had asked one to open and close one's mouth as quickly as he opened and closed his palms? He was very careful not to touch me physically, so there was nothing I could do, really, but avoid him. In reality, as I came to learn later, he was nice and gentle, playing the bully more than being the bully.

In the dorms, newcomers were *monos* and *jiggers*, to be put in their place, seen not heard. The worst bullies came from Form Two, doing to the freshmen what had been done to them the previous year. I found it strange that the most recent victims of bullying would be the worst perpetrators of that which they used to vehemently lament. I never understood the pleasure of humiliating another, least of all one weaker than oneself. I vowed that when I got to Form Two, I would not bully the newcomers, a promise to myself that I kept.

10

After some weeks, life settled into a routine. Monday to Friday were taken up by classes and other school-related activities. But on Saturday afternoons, after morning chores, many students added shoes and stockings to their uniform of khaki shorts and blue tie and left the school premises. Those who lived in the neighborhood went home, and the others would trek to the Indian shops at Kikuyu.

The town was originally a railway depot, set up in 1898, and as in similar depots, the Indians were the commercial frontiersmen, supplying the army of railroad workers and officials with food, clothes, and transport. The depot acquired a life of its own, which continued even after the railway construction had moved on.

I did not venture off the Alliance grounds in the first few weeks. I was not particularly eager to revisit Kikuyu station; I did not need a reminder of how I first came there smuggled on a goods train. But one Saturday, Wanjai and Leonard Mbũgua invited me to join them, and I felt it was time I dared to step out of the compound.

It was not a long walk. The legendary marshes of Ondiri were on our left, inducing in me the same awe I felt when reading and hearing stories about them. When we arrived in Kikuyu, our uniforms distinguished us from the rest of the population, as though the Indian shopkeepers and African shoppers were the natives to our explorers.

At the shopping center, however, I realized that our matching khaki hid a difference: I had followed Wanjai and the others blindly, thinking it was simply a walk to town, a bit of window shopping, and then another walk back. But when they started buying things, our equality fell apart. I did not have any money to spend and resorted to what I used to do in my previous schools when I had no lunch: I detached myself from the herd and went on my own. The shops looked like those in Limuru: draperies, with the owner behind the counter wearing a long tape measure around his neck; groceries, with the seller seated on a high stool, chewing leaves and ordering his assistants about; and others that specialized in varieties of food and candy arranged in bins. Even a cup of tea or the cheapest candy was beyond my means. I would have gone back to school, but I did not want to walk the distance alone.

Seeing some other freshmen walking toward me, holding their *mandazis* and other goodies, I ducked into the veranda of the nearest shop to let them pass. As I was about to go back into the street, a voice called out my name. I turned around, to find an African tailor smiling at me. I thought you were coming in just to greet me! he said as he shook my hand warmly. Don't you remember me? It was Igogo, the boy who had been teased out of school way back in our

Kamandũra days simply because his name meant Crow.*
He was now a man, a tailor, renting a Singer sewing machine
from the Indian shopkeeper and taking home his profits.
We chatted about the good old days, skirting around the
harassment that had driven him out of school. Your success
is ours as well, he told me, giving me coins to buy myself
something to eat, apologizing that he could not leave the
shop to join me. Whenever you are around, you must come
into the shop and tell me how you are, he said. Perhaps I
shall be free and then we can have tea together. I was truly
grateful. I bought some candy, and pride restored, I sought
out Wanjai and Mbũgua so we could walk back to school in
time for evening meal, the deadline for return.

Suddenly I saw people running away in all directions. I
had seen this before in Limuru: it was a raid. African soldiers under the command of their white officers, all armed
and in camouflage, jumped out of military jeeps that had
appeared from nowhere and ran after those disappearing
behind shops, shouting a menacing cacophonous mixture
of *Lala chini! Mikono juu!* Soon the raiders were all over
the small town, herding people into groups. But wonders
will never cease. Our Alliance uniform was a magic veil: the
hounds did not even seem to see us. Still, we felt safe only
after we were back in the sanctuary.

* I have told his story in *Dreams in a Time of War.*

I I

Life at school continued to be a series of discoveries. There was, for instance, the hierarchy and mystery of the prefect system, which was almost a mirror image of the colonial administration. The faculty may have been masters of our academic life, but it was through the prefects that the principal ruled the school. The senior class, successors and inheritors of those who had left last year, seemed to float on an intellectual cloud in an unattainable heaven. They walked, talked, and looked as if their bodies carried the weight of pure knowledge.

The deeds of those who had left, their antics, their exploits, their successes, even their very names, were the stuff of legends. Among those who had gone before us was Henry Kuria, who had written and directed a play in Kiswahili, *Nakupenda Lakini . . . I love you but . . .* The production, an all-students' affair, was first staged at Alliance and then taken to the community beyond. Kuria was also the founder and organizer of the Kĩambu Musical Festival for elementary schools in the district, and he accomplished all of this during the state of emergency.

It sounded like something out of a storybook, but the music festival had carried on after him and, in 1955, would be performed across the valley, at the Church of Torch. It was within walking distance, so I made the trip. The singing extravaganza by students uniformed in the different colors of the select elementary schools made a big impression on my mind. The legend himself was present as the guest of honor, but he sat too far in front for me to see him. It did not matter, though: he was real.

The 1955 festival was organized by Kuria's successor, Kĩmani Nyoike, now in his fourth year at Alliance. Kĩmani also followed in Kuria's literary footsteps by writing and producing a play, *Maisha ni Nini,* or *What Is Life?* performed to a boisterous full house in April. Already known for his debating skills, Kĩmani also played the leading role in his play. He was writer, orator, and actor, three talents in one body.

My previous experiences of staged performance were the improvised comic skits at Manguo Elementary School. *Maisha ni Nini,* the first full-length play I saw, was on a scale and level far beyond anything that I had previously encountered. Added to the Kuria legend, it was the foundation for my lifelong respect for students' efforts and for my own interest in theater.

12

First term was coming to a close, and I had already been changed immeasurably. Still, I did not quite feel that I belonged to Alliance. It was not only because the bullies continued to put us in our place at every opportunity; I also hadn't made a significant mark on anything. Intellectually, I was always mindful that the twenty others in the A stream had performed better than me, and even within my B stream, I could not tell where I stood. But despite this dislocation, I was caught by the fever that now seized the whole school. Exams! I did not have to be told that they were coming: I saw it in the sudden change of behavior. Students, everywhere, buried their heads in books, even the bullies.

My anxiety increased as Tuesday, April 5, the first day of exams, approached. After the last exam on Thursday, I felt even more crestfallen. The way the other boys talked of their performances discouraged me, especially when I compared the answers they so assertively claimed were correct with what I could recall of my own responses.

But when the results finally came, Henry Chasia, myself, and Hiram Karani, in that order, were at the top of both streams. I would move to A stream. The fact that I had done well in all subjects, even in the sciences, boosted my self-confidence. The students who had intimidated me, who could say, by rote, many of the theorems and formulas, had not done as well as their showy confidence had led me to expect.

So when the school assembly broke on April 21, the formal end of the first term, I had every reason to look forward to a triumphant return to my village. I felt differently about myself. My exam results had assured me that I was now truly an Alliance student. My uniform of khaki shorts and shirt, blue tie, shoes, and long socks announced the fact to the outside. The pass the school had issued me would confirm it to any inquisitive government agents. The image of bloodhounds panting at the gates, waiting to pounce on me, had faded into the background. Alliance would protect me from harm. Nothing prepared me, then, for the desolation of my village and the melancholy collection of mushrooms called Kamĩrĩthũ.

13

Villagization, the innocuous name the colonial state gave to the forced internal displacement, was sprung on the Kenyan people in 1955, in the middle of my first term at Alliance, but living within the walls of the school, I had not heard about the agents of the state bulldozing people's homes or torching them when the owners refused to participate in the demolition. Mau Mau suspects or not, everybody had to relocate to a common site. In some regions, the state forced people to dig a moat around the new collective settlement, leaving only one exit and entrance. The whole of central Kenya was displaced, and the old order of life destroyed, in the name of isolating and starving the anticolonial guerrillas in the mountains.

The mass relocation was followed by forced land consolidation. A person or families who owned parcels of land in different locations would have them joined together into a contiguous piece but had no choice over the location of this consolidated land. People in the mountains and the concentration camps were not there to verify their claims. It was a mass fraud, often giving land from the already poor to the relatively rich, and from the families of guerrilla fighters to those loyal to the colonial state.

Local Gĩkũyũ residents leaving Kamĩrĩthũ home guard post, having been forced there overnight for "protection" against Mau Mau attack, but really to prevent them from feeding Mau Mau fighters under the cover of night

The division between the loyal and everyone else was reflected in the architecture of the new village. The loyal occupied corner houses of corrugated iron roofs with ample space between them, while those deemed disloyal, the majority of the landless and poor, lived in mud-walled grass-thatched round huts, with hardly any space between them. The loyal household was likely to be Christian, relatively wealthy, better educated, with the nuclear family of father, mother, and children left intact. The peasant and worker households were usually just mothers and children.

The new villages were the rural equivalent of the concentration camps, where thousands were still being held, with more additions every year, since the Declaration of Emergency in 1952. The inmates of the concentration camps were mostly men, those in the concentration villages mostly women and children. These two sets of concentration had many features in common.

The most visible of these features was the watchtower, usually built on the highest ground, and from which the Union Jack fluttered its symbol of conquest and control. Under constant surveillance, the inmates of the camp and the village, loyal or not, were likely to be stopped and searched at any time of day or night. For all practical purposes, the line between the prison, the concentration camp, and the village had been erased.

14

In the new Kamĩrĩthũ, my family lived in a mud hut, with our bedding on the floor. I don't know how my mother managed to organize some semblance of meals. Only on certain hours of given days could women attend their fields or work for the wealthier villagers. My sister, Njoki, and my brother's wife, Charity, now and then worked on the European-owned tea estates.

Adding to the melancholy was the talk of a doomsday. In mid-January 1955, Governor Sir Evelyn Baring had offered amnesty to any Mau Mau guerrillas who would surrender. This offer followed the failure of the 1954 surrender negotiations under Operation General China. Under the terms of the amnesty, just as in the failed negotiations of late 1954, the guerrillas would get not a single concession to their political demands for land and freedom, but a pledge of prison instead of gallows. In both situations, the colonial state refused to see the Mau Mau as a legitimate anticolonial nationalist movement with political goals. Low-flying airplanes dropped leaflets in the mountains and villages, threatening unspecified consequences should the guerrillas not accept the offer. The threats intensified amid the building of the new village.

I viewed the offer and the threats as they related to my elder brother, Good Wallace, who fought somewhere in the mountains. I feared for his life. Throughout the break, the doomsday scenario hung over our family, made worse, for me at least, by the fact that we did not really talk about it. I was a little surprised to see Charity, my brother's wife, taking the threats of doom so calmly, but maybe she was just putting on a front. Packed with so much anxiety and uncertainty, my three weeks of break ended without my having met with Kenneth to discuss his book.

I went back to Alliance on May 12 to begin my second term in the sanctuary, haunted by images of the community prison I had helped to build back home, and weighed down by thoughts of the doom awaiting Good Wallace and his fellow guerrillas for defying the calls to surrender. Henceforth I was going to live out my life in a home that reminded me of the loss of home and a school that offered shelter but not the certainty of home. Both, ironically, were colonial constructs, but I feared that even they might clash at any moment and crush my dreams.

15

Edward Carey Francis had been on leave when I first arrived at Alliance in January, but his absence was strongly felt. Boys in classes ahead of us talked about him as a mystery. They called him Hiuria or Kihiuria, conjuring the image of a big rhino on the offensive and its sideways motion when turning. He was usually a reference point in stories about Alliance. Everywhere, in dorms during the hours of rest, in the dining hall at mealtimes, in classes between lessons, the older students would talk about what they thought had become loose or too relaxed since Carey Francis went on leave to England in December 1954. Of the teachers' wives, who wore colorful dresses, especially on Sundays, the students said that they were behaving with the abandon of children in the absence of their stern father. *Paka akienda Panya hutawala*, others would say in Kiswahili. Wait and see what the mice will do when the cat comes back. Sometimes the students would imitate Carey Francis's walks under different moods, particularly when he caught a teacher or a student doing something of which he disapproved. Alarmingly, they claimed that none could escape his notice: he knew every single boy in the school, all two hundred of them, by name. No, he knew the names of all the boys who had ever gone through Alliance since he assumed its leadership in 1940. In my imagination, he became a huge formless unknown.

Early in the second term, as Wanjai, Aaron Kandie, Kirui, and I were walking from the dining room after lunch, I saw a figure, dressed in a khaki safari-type coat, shorts, and stockings, walking in the sun across the fields, playing with a dog: he would throw a tennis-size ball as far as he could, and the dog would run and retrieve it. That is Hiuria, Wanjai told me. Carey Francis, the others chimed in. He had come back from England on May 21, nine days after my return from break. He did not look like the scary figure of my imagination. You just wait, Wanjai said.

Immediately the effects of his return could be felt and seen. A new alacrity, timing, and self-discipline were discernible among faculty and students, as if they did not want to risk being caught wrong-footed. Still, I could not tell what the fuss was all about.

And then one Sunday, during a morning parade before chapel, I saw for myself the fury that fueled the tales. The parade started rather inauspiciously. Carey Francis, dressed in a gray suit and blue tie, stood in front of us, as did the other teachers and their wives. As we waited for the inspection ritual, a European couple, Mr. and Mrs. Kingsnorth, a bit late, passed by him. Mrs. Kingsnorth wore a dress with a hemline that revealed a bit of her legs, more so than the other ladies. The scent of her perfume filled the air.

Suddenly Carey Francis started breathing heavily through the nose, fuming, tongue thrust into the cheek, rolling it side to side inside his closed mouth, as if moving a small ball from one side to the other, so that his left and right cheeks swelled in turn. He started stumping, left, then right, to and fro, sometimes in small circles, like, I had to admit, a bull about to charge, each step raising dust that expressed his rage, his trousers swaying, as if equally furious. Students called it stepping. For a moment, I thought the ground underneath his feet would give way. Surprisingly, the faculty and older students seemed nonplussed, as if they had seen this before and were simply waiting for the storm to pass or at least subside.

On this occasion, it did not end the way they thought it would. His heavy breathing and stepping were echoed in the sky by thunder, lightning, and a sudden downpour. The prefects tried to maintain a disciplined march to the chapel, but soon they, and even the teachers and their wives, had to follow the mass of boys running toward the holy shelter. With everybody finally seated in their pews, a perfectly calm Carey Francis read a passage from *Pilgrim's Progress* in which Christian, while visiting the Interpreter's House, is taken into a parlor full of dust. As the room is being swept, the flying dust almost chokes the onlookers. Then a woman sprinkles water on the floor and all is well:

Then said Christian: What means this? The Interpreter answered: This parlor is the heart of a man that was never sanctified by the sweet grace of the gospel. The dust is his original sin and inward corruptions that have defiled the man. He that began to sweep at first is the Law; but she that brought water and did sprinkle it is the gospel.

Out of this, Carey Francis gave an incredible performance in which he likened Alliance to the Interpreter's House, where the dust we had brought from the outside could be swept away by the law of good behavior and watered by the gospel of Christian service. The word *service* peppered the entire sermon. But, he added, it was only Jesus, through mercy, who could grace the outcome of our earthly struggles.

The sermon from the chapel seemed a fitting follow-up to nature's sermon in the storm. But it was the Franciscan fury preceding both that became the topic of conversation. What had triggered it? It was the tardy couple, some said. Carey Francis hated tardiness and wanted teachers to set a good example. No, others countered, it was the woman's perfume, her dress, the hemline. He does not like excess. No, not excess: he has a thing about women. His ways are at odds with the norm, don't you think? others asked, extending the talk beyond the fury and the sermon to his whole life. How could he abandon a prestigious position as a university lecturer in mathematics at Cambridge to accept a lowly one as headmaster of a primary school in Africa in 1928? You think it's just a missionary call to service? No, it was something else. Very personal. Oh, yes. Thwarted love.

During the First World War, the story went, Carey Francis fought in England and France. But when he returned home, he found his sweetheart had gone to sweeten the life of another. He turned his broken heart away from women to his dog and God, the only two who could never abandon him, and he turned his resourceful mind away from the serene life of a don on grass lawns in Cambridge to one of self-sacrifice and pure devotion in the thorny bushes of Africa. Fact or fiction, the story of love and war seemed to make sense in explaining how this man, born in Hampstead, London, on September 13, 1897, educated at William Ellis School and Trinity College, Cambridge, senior wrangler in the Mathematics Tripos, would leave everything behind for a dusty elementary school in a foreign land to start a new life from nothing.

Carey Francis came to Alliance in 1940, a kind of war-time principal, where he started by imposing strict discipline. He did not like the lax ways of Grieves's ancien régime and vowed to overthrow it and reconstruct Alliance in his image. Under the new regime, everything was going to change drastically, as in a revolution, the first act being the replacement of the students' knee-length khaki shorts, maroon fez, and black tassels with plain khaki shorts and shirts. He expelled teachers, especially Africans, who would not fall in line. Others simply left in protest. The students grumbled over the loss of their teachers and even more over the loss of their maroon fez and black tassels. But the breaking point between the new principal and the students came over the Franciscan call for them to grow vegetables in allotted gardens to contribute to the British war effort. Someone removed the notice the new principal had put up, and no student would own up to the impudence or snitch on another.

Carey Francis responded with a mixture of expulsions and caning, the boys readmitted, on a one-by-one basis, only after each of them accepted in writing that they were wrong, promised to obey the new rules of discipline, and said thank you sir for the punishment. He used the crisis to reorganize the day-to-day running of the school by separating the academic from the administrative, and the classroom from the dorm: teachers would still be in charge of curricula and related activities, but the student prefect system would handle student life outside the classroom. The principal was, of course, the head of both the academic and the administrative hierarchies. The legend of a disciplinarian was born, to mingle in school lore with stories of love and war and magic.

Once, while taking a walk through one of the villages not far from Alliance, Carey Francis stopped to chat with a crowd of African children. He asked a boy to let him see the coin he was holding. With all their eyes on him, Carey Francis made the coin disappear and then reappear behind the ear of another boy. The children did not wait for more but streamed home to tell about the magic and the man.

One Saturday evening I saw the full display of his magic. I could not believe that the person on the stage was the stern principal I thought I knew. Time and again he made cards and golf balls disappear into thin air and then reappear, seemingly from nowhere. Most startling were the rabbits and doves he pulled from his hat. But at the end of it, perhaps mindful of the village incident, he was careful to explain that he was playing magic, not practicing it: his acts were conjuring tricks. It was my first experience of such tricks, and whenever, in later years, I witnessed more amazing conjuring feats from professional magicians, I always recalled that first Night of Magic with Edward Carey Francis at Alliance.

What I would later have no doubts about was his magic as a reader. During one of his Friday assemblies, he introduced us to a book, *Three Men in a Boat (To Say Nothing of the Dog)*, by Jerome K. Jerome, an account of a boating trip on the Thames River. At first I was skeptical: who wanted to hear of boats on rivers that one had not seen? But when he started to read, I suddenly found myself engrossed in the humorous trials and tribulations, including the drama of making an Irish stew out of unpeeled potatoes, a cabbage, half a peck of peas, half a pork pie, a bit of cold boiled bacon, potted salmon, and other leftovers.

By the time he finished the excerpts, I felt part of the imaginary boat ride on a river I did not know, laughing. It was a moment more magical than the night of conjuring tricks. I found it difficult to reconcile the images of the tongue-eating, stumping conjurer of storms; the tongue-in-cheek conjurer of illusions; and this loose-tongued conjurer of life from a book published in 1889.

16

Carey Francis did not teach the lower forms. He remained a towering figure who was everywhere, who could generate fury, fire, and fun in turns. I would have liked to know him as a teacher, but I had to make do with the occasional sermon in the chapel and the Friday assemblies, during which he would discuss current affairs, national, continental, and international, his way of keeping in touch with the entire student community.

Winston Churchill's resignation from his Conservative prime ministership in November was the subject of such an assembly soon after Carey Francis returned from leave. Churchill was one of the leading statesmen in the world. Even the fact that throughout his career he had changed parties was a testament to his independent character: he was more loyal to principles than to parties. By keeping his head cool when all about him were losing theirs, Churchill had rallied the world to defeat Hitler. He offered *blood, toil, tears, and sweat*, where a scoundrel would have promised Heaven. His alliance with President Franklin D. Roosevelt to sign the Atlantic Charter in 1941, in a secret meeting on the British battleship HMS *Prince of Wales*, had changed the aims of the war from just a victory over Hitler to one for human freedom, reaffirming people's right to choose the government under which they lived.

Churchill's words came across with such force of conviction that it was easy to be carried away by his assertions. But inside me was always the cautionary voice of Ngandi*, my beloved mentor of earlier years, who had drawn a different picture of Churchill: as a fighter for the preservation of the empire. Ngandi had complained of Churchill's ingratitude in allowing Governor Baring to declare a state of emer-

---

* See *Dreams in a Time of War.*

gency in Kenya and send British troops to crush the very Kenyans who had helped him fight Hitler and now wanted freedom. It was Churchill's Conservatives who reproduced, in Kenya, Hitler's concentration camps. Ngandi might have disappeared from my life, but his way of looking at the world, questioning the assertive correctness of authority, stayed with me. I did not need Ngandi's presence to add to the list of imperial evils in the concentration villages all over central Kenya, for I had just come back from one. Churchill had caused me to lose my home. The loss lurked inside me, stoking fears of more unexpected and sudden interruptions of my life. Governor Baring's doomsday, the day he demanded the Mau Mau surrender or else, set for June 10, hung over my second term at Alliance, made heavier by the fact that I could not share my anxieties about Good Wallace with anybody.

However, the drama of daily life and learning at school was enough to distract me from thoughts of the new village, the doomsday, and my brother in the mountains. By August 4, when the second term ended and I returned to the village for break, the doomsday had come and gone. But it had hit my home: my mother had been detained in the home guard post for questioning. She talked very little about the ordeal she had undergone, and I felt sure that there were many more things my family hid from me, to save me from the burden of knowing what they knew. They treated me as an outsider who could not bear too much reality. In protecting me, they made my estrangement much harder to overcome.

Suspects rounded up by British soldiers during a sweep through part of Nairobi's Eastlands, 1953

Though its propaganda planes stopped dropping leaflets, the state intensified bombings on Mount Kenya, conducted arbitrary raids in towns and rural marketplaces, and carried out mass arrests and public hangings. This had happened so regularly that the new village seemed to have incorporated them into an eerie semblance of normality. But the normality did not lessen the melancholy that seemed captured in the blue canopy of smoke hovering over the huts.

I returned to school for the third and last term of my first year on August 4. There was a slight change in the staff, with the departure of Allan Ogot and his replacement by a new teacher, A. Kilelu. Classes would continue as before, but this change threatened the stability that I had hoped for in the sanctuary.

17

The third term did not carry the curiosity and expectation of my first arrival, or the Franciscan drama of the second term, but I could now see the light at the end of the tunnel of my freshman status. The existential condition of always being merely tolerated by older students would end and their bullying along with it. The exam fever, more intense than at any time before, emphasized the coming of the end. For me, I felt the pressure, going into the second year, to keep my place among the top ten in stream A. I was not looking forward to the end of the year or leaving the premises, even for a few weeks, but the intensity of preparation for exams took my thoughts away from the hounds waiting outside the gate.

The prep rooms were always packed, the grounds full of students reading under the shade of trees. More and more students were caught trying to read by the light of their flashlights under their blankets when they were supposed to be sleeping. The school had turned into a space for bookworms. It came as a surprise, then, when I learned that rehearsals of Shakespeare's *As You Like It* were going on, that even some seniors were involved.

The Alliance dramatic society had been founded in 1939, and Shakespeare became an annual fixture in the 1950s, with *Henry V* in 1952, *Macbeth* in 1953, and *Julius Caesar* in 1954, productions that had become part of the school's lore. The older students told of Joseph Mũngai's role as Macbeth with awe, that when he left the stage after the line *Is this a dagger which I see before me,* he was shaking as if he still held the bloodstained weapon. After the performance, he was in tears, as if he could see blood everywhere. For a week afterward, he kept to himself, still in character, haunted by the blood of his victims.

Mũngai had already graduated from Alliance and gone to Makerere University College, but his Macbeth had left a mark, perhaps even inspiring Moses Gathere's mornings of *Had I but died an hour,* which had once startled me. I looked forward to the forthcoming *As You Like It,* hoping, vaguely, for similar drama on and off the stage. The dining hall had been changed into an auditorium with chairs facing the stage, itself transformed, with a proscenium extension. Arden did indeed look like a forest through which the actors in their rich colorful costumes wandered. Boys played both male and female roles, as in Shakespeare's time. It was fascinating to see dresses, earrings, and head scarves turn boys into beautiful ladies of the court. Equally fascinating though strange was the sight of Africans dressed in sixteenth-century English costumes, speaking in iambic pentameter.

But what the performance lacked in social authenticity or anything resembling local history, it more than made up for as a spectacle of other histories, far away and long ago. When I heard Mwangi Kamunge, as the melancholy Jaques, say: *All the world's a stage, and all the men and women merely players: They have their exits and their entrances; and one man in his time plays many parts,* I had a momentary vision of the world as a vast village of the old type with numerous paths, their entries and exits beyond the horizon.

As I followed the action, just about everything I saw and heard, from scenery, to lines delivered, to dress and gait, triggered my imagination. I could not help comparing the pairs of exiles in Arden to my brother, Good Wallace, wandering in the forests of Nyandarwa and Mount Kenya or wherever in the mountains he now lived. I could imagine the guerrillas carving coded messages for each other or reading the pamphlets dropped from the sky. But my mental meanderings did not take away from my overall enjoy-

A scene from Alliance High School's 1955 production
of Shakespeare's *As You Like It*

ment of this first experience of staged Shakespeare. Maybe the play's happy ending could portend . . . but dwelling on that possibility raised the other possibility.

Thoughts and images of my guerrilla brother often stole into my mind at the most unexpected times, triggered by any association, but most often by Oades. Ever since he had taken us to his house for our first English lesson, I could not forget that, as a member of the Kenya Police Reserve, he could have come into a deadly face-to-face with my brother. Oades was a kindly person, and I could not imagine him in a shoot-out with anybody, but when I learned that he would return to England in December, I felt some relief.

My first annual speech day was an extravaganza of guests, speeches, and prizes, formally announcing the end of my first year at Alliance. All of us in our class had to chase Henry Chasia, but I had successfully maintained my position among the top. I would carry this success back to my mother. She might not understand the differences between A and B streams, but I would assure her that I had done my best.

The holidays began on December 10. It was incredible how people had adjusted to their new life in the concentration village, at least on the surface. I would try to do likewise. My younger brother, Njinjũ, was my regular companion, and he knew all the ways of the new narrow streets. He and I would take *panga* and *jembe* and walk to the fields to join my mother. On these treks, the women would stare in disbelief: an Alliance student was going to dirty his educated hands in the fields. But the dirt actually helped me adjust. The fields my mother cultivated were largely the same ones she always had, and while working there, pulling out the weeds, mulching, clearing bush, and eating her fire-roasted potatoes, I would feel a sense of connection with the old, with what had been lost. On my return to the village in the evening, melancholy would steal back into me, but inside the hut, with memories of work in the fields and the occasional story, I would experience the illusion of the old homestead, an illusion soon shredded by reality.

Just before Christmas, my brother's wife, Charity, was arrested, accused of organizing food and clothes for the guerrillas in the mountains. I had never seen her collect food or clothes; there were not even enough to go around in our home, and I did not see how she could have found the time. But now my brother was out in the mountains, and my sister-in-law was in the notorious Kamĩtĩ Maximum Security Prison. Yes, reality had stolen joy from my Christmas.

1956

A Tale of Souls in Conflict

18

I could hardly wait for January 18, 1956, to return to the sanctuary. In my first year, the outside had not intruded except that every member of the Gĩkũyũ, Embu, and Meru communities had to have a written permit to travel by train or any public transport from one region to another, the lack of which had almost derailed my first entry into the school. Otherwise, the permit played no role in life inside the sanctuary. But in my second year, the outside began to make itself felt within the walls.

We had hardly settled down when some government officials came to the school to take fingerprints. We were required to have identity cards. Every time I saw the officials, I felt my stomach tighten. The whole process went smoothly, but the colonial policies were changing so fast that the ID card was soon out of date, to be replaced by a passbook, an internal passport like those in apartheid South Africa. Every movement across regions by a member of the affected communities was to be stamped on its pages. The bar for getting the document was raised: a recipient had to be thoroughly screened and certified that he had not taken an oath of allegiance to the Mau Mau. In March 1956 an official screening team visited the school and for two weeks

Members of Livingstone House, 1956: House Master David Martin
(second row center), Assistant House Master Ben Ogutu (next to Martin
in the middle), Ngũgĩ (first row standing, second from right)

interviewed teachers, students, and staff of Gĩkũyũ, Embu, and Meru origins. When my turn came, it was determined that I should be screened in Limuru and would have to bring back a stamped letter from the district office, certifying my innocence. To get the stamp, I would have to get a letter of clearance from the chief of my location. This would have to be done during the term break.

So instead of enjoying my new life as a second-year student, I felt my sanctuary haunted by fear of failing the clearance. The chief that I had left behind was reputed to be cruel. He would know about my brother being in the mountains and his wife being in prison. I did not see how he would give me a clean bill of political health, and the fear nagged me, dogged me. I did not have anybody in whom I could confide. Though Wanjai and I both came from Limuru, our families were on opposite sides in the anti-colonial struggle.

I once came very close to sharing my burden with Samuel Githegi. Githegi and I were classmates, and we often exchanged pleasantries. He had a warm personality and was friends with many people. But there was something about him, a kind of sadness or loneliness, that I could not then understand. Once, after lunch, we walked out together and wandered about in the yard. I was about to tell him of my fears when, out of the blue, he started talking about sugar. Apparently he had what he called a sugar illness. It was serious, he said, but even then I could not understand: diabetes was not in our vocabulary, and he looked the very picture of good health. The sad strain behind his friendly face prevented me from talking about myself.*

I thought of my teachers. How would they receive the information about my family? They might turn me in as the brother of a Mau Mau guerrilla. My coming of age had been shaped by the notion of a white monolith, *Mbarĩ ya Nyakerũ*, pitted against a black monolith, *Mbarĩ ya Nyakairũ*. Every popular song had talked about it. The very identity of the land was contested: White Highlands versus

---

* A year or so after leaving Alliance High School, Githegi succumbed to diabetes.

Ngũgĩ (on right) and Samuel Githegi (on left), outside on
Alliance High School grounds

Black People's Land.* Jomo Kenyatta, who would become
the first Kenyan president, had once written of Kenya as
a *Bũrũri wa Ngũĩ*, Land of Conflict. Black and white conflict, of course. Who, really, were these whites who held
the chalk and seemed completely dedicated to our mental
welfare? And who were these blacks teaching alongside the
whites and equally dedicated to our mental welfare? Where
did they fit in the schema of white versus black?

Even amid the horrors of war, concentration camps, and
villages, the few African teachers at Alliance had remained
positive models of what we could become, but they often

* In 1902, Sir Charles Eliot, governor of colonial Kenya, had set aside the
prime estate of Limuru as part of the White Highlands, for Europeans only.
Black Africans were relegated to the less desirable land, labeled African
Reserves.

did not last long enough for us to know them well. Joseph Kariuki was the most constant black presence. He was an old boy, who had entered Alliance in 1945, becoming school captain in 1949 before going to Makerere, which had just become a degree-awarding Overseas College of the University of London. He was among the first, the lucky thirteen, to earn a degree at Makerere in 1954. His personality endeared him to everyone, and even Carey Francis seemed a little more tolerant in his case. Kariuki made a spectacle when he played lawn tennis with white ladies on Saturday afternoons, teachers from the girls' school. He and the ladies were dressed in white, he in his shorts and tennis shoes, and they in similar shoes but with skirts whose hemlines were far above their knees. After a game, Kariuki could be seen trekking back to his house with his white female tennis partner. It may have been because Carey Francis himself was an avid tennis and croquet player, but I noted no outburst from him. Charming and debonair, Kariuki used to push the envelope in other ways, and when left in charge of the school as the master on duty on the weekend, he would show us films with exciting secular themes that other teachers would not show.

Though he taught lawn tennis and literature, his real passion was music. It was not a subject in itself, but arguing that music was the gateway to literature, particularly poetry, he would play European classics, Beethoven, Mozart, and Bach, at every opportunity, provoking skeptical laughter when he said that Beethoven wrote his Ninth Symphony, with the "Ode to Joy" movement, while completely deaf and in poor health. If he was really deaf, how could he hear the music he wrote? Feeling, Kariuki would say. He felt it in his heart and mind. Music vibrates in the mind before it is captured in sound. Shut your eyes and think of a familiar melody: can't you hear soundless motion?

Kariuki was also in charge of the school choir, and it was in the spiritual that he most excelled in bringing together music and poetry. Because of the school's roots in the American South model, the spiritual had always been popular at Alliance, but Kariuki took it to another level. Though he did not dwell too much on the politics of the spiritual, he talked about its background as a survival mechanism on the slave plantation, letting the music speak to us directly through its own language. The sheer force of his energy and enthusiasm turned even the most skeptical into musical believers and unbridled enthusiasts for the spiritual. Whether Kariuki intended the effect or not, the spiritual's poetry of resistance and music of liberation eloquently echoed in a Kenya then governed under the state of emergency. How could one hear the school choir, which he led, sing, *Oh freedom, over me, and before I'll be a slave, I'll be buried in my grave, and go home to my Lord and be free,* and not feel the yearning for freedom around us?

Perhaps I could unburden myself to Kariuki. He would understand. But neither in the classroom nor outside did he openly discuss the parallels between the music and the terror in the country. Neither did we. We kept our thoughts to ourselves, confining our musings to matters of meter and melody.

19

In general, the Alliance classroom of our times abstracted knowledge from local reality. It had not been always so. The early years had seen bold attempts to relate the vocational side of the school to local knowledge. Agriculture was then a major subject, and studies of indigenous trees and fruits, the language of cattle marks, beekeeping, and butter making were part of the classroom. Efforts to connect with local technology included visits to local blacksmiths, from whom the students learned how to make forges and smelt iron. Teachers were required to learn at least one African language, and the program of Bantu studies and civics incorporated a practical project of recording African legends, riddles, proverbs, and songs.

But as the literary side of the academy gradually took over, the tribute to local knowledge diminished. With Makerere, in 1948, beginning to offer degree programs from the University of London, secondary education became increasingly a preparation for college, with the Overseas Cambridge School Certificate the gateway to academic heaven. By the time I joined the school in 1955, hardly any traces, except in carpentry, remained of these early efforts to mine and harvest local knowledge.

Our literature classes were no different: English texts were the norm, and Europe the cultural reference. But Kariuki, who took over from James Smith in 1956, introduced fun into the study of literature. To Shakespeare's *Macbeth*, the set text, he added what he called love sonnets, which we happily welcomed, thinking they might turn out to be useful to hearts awakening to Cupid's whispers, real or imagined. One boy in fact soon claimed that he had used Shakespeare's eighteenth sonnet on an Acrossian one sunny afternoon, with unspecified good results.

In the first term of my first year, the constant allusions to Acrossians in tales told by seniors had puzzled me. The name conjured an image of dwellers from a different planet, who would occasionally descend to play in a valley of green meadows awash with magic that lured men. Wanjai unraveled the mystery of the valley to me.

In its early years, Alliance High School, though mostly for boys, also admitted girls. Among its earliest female graduates was Nyokabi, who later married her teacher, Eliud Mathu, himself the second Kenyan African to get a B.A., the first African to join the staff of Alliance, the first African to represent African interests in the Legislative Council, and the first African member of the colonial Executive Council. Among the last female graduates was Rebecca Njau, an actress of amazing power and grace in the 1951 Alliance production of *The Lady with a Lamp*, who, years later, would become a force in women's education and a pioneering novelist, playwright, and internationally acclaimed batik artist. Still, the number of female students had remained small: between the first intake in 1938 and the last in 1952, the school had averaged only five girls annually.

The situation of women in secondary education changed

when a separate Alliance Girls High School was officially opened in 1948. The two institutions literally faced each other across a valley, so the students referred to dwellers in the opposite institution as Acrossians. For the boys, their female counterparts were nymphs in a misty valley who sang soft but irresistible siren songs, melodies wrought with a promise to mellow the souls of the lucky and, equally, with a danger of anguishing the unlucky. Nearly every tale that related to matters of the heart started and ended with reference to these nymphs, and one did not always know what to believe. But now, here in the second year, one of us swore that he had emerged from the green meadow with the promise and not the anguish, all on account of a Shakespearean sonnet. The success spurred us on. We committed the whole sonnet to memory and could be heard reciting it loudly in the school corridors, trying out different poses and voice modulations: *Shall I compare thee to a summer's day? / Thou art more lovely and more temperate,* and then declaim, *Thy eternal summer shall not fade / Nor lose possession of that fair thou owest,* clinching the performance with the last two lines:

> So long as men can breathe, or eyes can see,
> So long lives this, and this gives life to thee.

Though I never tested the sonnet's effect on any Acrossian, the words were no less sweet, particularly when performed by Kariuki himself. He read them with a flair that brought out their drama and music. With the sonnets, Kariuki made a case for the immortality of literary creations: in a classroom in Kenya in 1956, we were reading words written somewhere in Stratford-upon-Avon or on the streets of London by a bard who died in 1616.

20

But even Kariuki could not make me passionate about three centuries of English obsession with flowers and seasons. In Kenya there was sunshine and green life all year round, and flowers were never a thing of surprise. I could not escape the magic of literature, its endless ability to elicit laughter, tears, a whole range of emotions, but the fact that these emotions were exclusively rooted in the English experience of time and place could only add to my sense of dislocation. Not every flower in the world was one of Wordsworth's *host of golden daffodils.* Kenya's flora and fauna, and the rainy and dry seasons, could also provide images that captured the timeless relevance of art, but we did not encounter them in class.

This tendency to make Europe the reference point for human experience was exacerbated by the content and approaches in other subjects as well. In geography, the European landscape, mountains, rivers, and industrial locations were the primary formations to which the African versions, secondary of course, could now be contrasted. To the River Thames, about which I learned in my elementary schooling, I added knowledge of the other *civilized* waters in Europe—the Seine, Danube, Rhine, and Rubicon—as the early locations of commerce and trade. African rivers—the Niger, Nile, Congo, and Zambesi—all discovered by Europeans, had any number of reasons for not being sites of civilization, except of course the Nile Delta, but even that was really part of the Mediterranean and Asia Minor, as the Middle East was then named.

In history class, we traveled through sixteenth- and seventeenth-century England, admiring a gallery of dashing heroes. Even African history was largely the story of Europeans in Africa. Livingstone, Stanley, Speke, and Burton were the larger-than-life bearers of light to a Dark Continent. They were soul merchants, traversing terrains of dangerous forests clad in nothing more than the Bible, spreading enlightenment and casting out the devil. In the story of colonial settlements in Africa and America, only the Spanish and German rivals wallowed in blood, while the English overcame challenges of nature and man. Even in the story of the slave trade, the English, with their antislavery legal enactments, emerged as the heroes of the abolition movement and not the villains of its earlier expansion.

Brilliant in many ways and able to evoke the dramas of history, our teachers, like those in other schools, were following a syllabus laid out by the Cambridge Examination Board. I don't believe they deliberately distorted the story; they simply offered their objective history of Africa from an imperialist point of view. We crammed the notes, facts, viewpoints, and all because, even then we understood that the correct answers to the often-biased questions determined the future. Our future was made in England.

This pedagogy may have had some unintended benefits:

the glamour of the far away and long ago contrasted sharply with the gloom of the near and present. An escape into wintry snow, flowers of spring, mountain chalets, and piracy on the high seas of those times and places carried my mind away from the anxieties of the moment.

But whatever their fascination, these images of the past could not hold off time. The school vacation finally started on May 10, which for me revived the fear that this could be my last day at Alliance: I would not be allowed back without a clean bill of political health.

21

For the first few days of the break, I put off the inevitable confrontation with the chief. Hinga had succeeded his sadistic brother, Ragae, who had been assassinated under dramatic circumstances. Mau Mau agents had stalked him from Limuru market and shot him. They did not kill him, but much later, disguised as hospital assistants, they followed him to Kĩambu hospital and shot him dead through a pillow they used as a silencer. Though Chief Hinga did not exhibit the same level of cruelty as his brother, I assumed that he must harbor resentments against his brother's assassins. As the end of the break approached, I decided to be done with it, but not without much agonizing. Would he require me to go before yet another screening team to prove that I had not taken the oath? How could I prove that, here in the new Kamĩrĩthũ, where everybody knew about Good

Wallace? The chief was sure to be prejudiced against the brother of a Mau Mau guerrilla fighter.

It was a lonely walk through the narrow streets of the village, to the military post, built on the highest part of the ridge. As I approached the gate, I felt its threatening watchtower looming larger and larger over me. Since its construction in 1954, the post had been a site of torture, its walls built to muffle the cries and moans of the victims. My mother had been incarcerated there for three months answering questions about my brother's disappearance and again afterward, from time to time, at the whims of the powers.

Suddenly, from apparently nowhere, I heard a command: halt. After an eerie silence, the drawbridge was lowered. My stomach was very tight as I walked over it. Under the bridge was a cavernous moat covered with barbed wire and jutted with sharp wooden spikes. At the gate, armed with papers and my school uniform, I made my purpose known, and they let me in. Home guards and administrative police, guns slung over their shoulders, moved about the yard, with others cleaning their guns or playing dice or checkers. Still others, wearing vests for shirts, put their clothes on the lines to dry. I was inside an armed camp, my sole protective armor being the Alliance uniform I wore. I was taken to the chief's office, in the administrative square building with walls of stone and an iron roof.

I could not believe my eyes. The new chief was Fred Mbũgua, Kenneth's father, my old teacher at Manguo Elementary who had once noticed and praised my composition.

A fortified home guard post, at Kiajogu in Nyeri District,
with watchtower and staked moat

There had been a recent change, apparently, and the illiterate chief had been replaced by one with formal schooling. I did not know what to make of my old teacher as a colonial chief, I was just glad that he did not ask me any questions, simply writing a letter in his clear cursive stating that I had been screened and found not to have taken the oath. I was elated as I left the office and the precinct, even when I realized that although he had signed the letter, he had not marked it with an official stamp. Regardless, I still had to make an expedition to Tigoni district assistant's office for the final official confirmation of my political cleanliness.

Tigoni police station, the location of the regional district office, was a few miles from Limuru township, past Loreto Girls School, in an area where Europeans and Africans claimed the same lands, White Highlands to the former, Black People's Country to the latter. The entrance to the district assistant's office was a couple yards after the main entrance, and I joined the line waiting for service. Other people came and stood behind me, forming a long queue, and two police officers saw to it that people did not jump the line.

My turn finally came. A white officer sat behind the desk, bending over a folder. A black police officer, a rifle by his side, stood near him, looking at me suspiciously, as if my Alliance uniform were a fake. Eventually the white officer raised his eyes. He looked young but put on a grave face, performing authority. In my mind, I named him Johnny the Green, *Johnny* being the generic reference we used for British soldiers. I handed him my Alliance papers and the chief's document that affirmed my innocence. He glanced at the documents and the letter in silence, then looked at me askance, wondering why I brought him documents that simply confirmed that I was from Alliance and had not taken the oath. I explained, haltingly, that the letter needed his official seal, a requirement before I could be issued a passport. He glanced at it again, took a stamp on the table, and applied it, but as he was about to hand the document back to me, he stopped and looked at it yet again. He must have realized that it was not written on the chief's letterhead and certainly did not carry the chief's seal. He gave me the document with the order: Wait outside. You'll be screened again.

This was the end of the road for me, I thought. There was no way I was going to pass the bar before a white stranger or the police officers he would ask to screen me. I stood on the veranda for a while. For some reason, none of the officers seemed unduly bothered with me. I even tried making eye contact, without any discernible response. They were clearly more concerned with those in line than with me. I faced a dilemma: wait and fail the screening or walk away and risk arrest. The document with the official seal was in my pocket. Why wait?

I started moving backward, a step at a time, and nobody attempted to stop me. Two. Three. Four. I was now off the veranda, outside. I turned my back to the building and walked, slowly, unhurriedly, onto the track that led to the main road. I turned left, past the main entrance to the police station. I decided, if caught and taken back to the office, to swear that I had not understood Johnny the Green's English accent, but the mere thought of being caught broke my armor of carefully cultivated insouciance. Suddenly panic seized me. I heard footsteps. Sirens? Gunfire? Sweat broke out. I started running, not daring to look back to confirm, and did not stop until I was back in Kamĩrĩthũ. The pursuing footsteps, the sirens, and the sounds of gunfire had been in my mind only.

22

Back at Alliance at the beginning of August, and now possessing a clean bill of political health, I was issued my passbook. The passbook aimed to further tighten government control of the movement of the Gĩkũyũ, Embu, and Meru communities in the entire country, and to put a wedge between their members and non-GEM Africans. Not even our teachers were exempt.

By giving the illusion that some communities were more privileged, the state hoped to buy their loyalty. But in reality, when it came to sudden raids, blackness, not passbooks, was the uniform profile and identity of the suspect. It was only after the raids that IDs would help sort out the GEMs and non-GEMs. And by then all would have suffered some form of harassment and humiliation.

At Alliance, life was back to normal. But the passbook confirmed that the seemingly unconnected rhythms of life in the school, the country, and the world would sometimes cross and impact our lives in the sanctuary directly, making me realize that perhaps the boundary I had assumed to exist between them, like the pursuing sirens of my escape, had all along been in my mind only.

At any rate, it was clear, by mid-1956, that the rest of my life at Alliance would be a series of crossings between the conflicting realities of the school and the new village. I was coming to terms with the awareness that whatever relief the sanctuary offered me was not permanent, that both locations, Alliance and Kamĩrĩthũ, would always remind me of loss. Incrementally, I also resolved that even in times of fear, I must not succumb to fear completely. The venture inside the Kamĩrĩthũ home guard post, all alone, and my later instinctive escape from Johnny the Green, stoked the nascent defiance within me, urging me to dare outside the walls of the sanctuary, even during term time, despite the hounds at the gate. It was such a crossing, one too many, that eventually earned me a summons to the principal's office for my first face-to-face encounter with Edward Carey Francis.

23

On one special Saturday, students were free to be away from the compound all day, provided they returned to school by six. It was called Nairobi Saturday, probably because many students, particularly those who came from distant places and therefore could not go home, went to the capital city instead. In the first year, I did not take advantage of Nairobi Saturday; my experiences during the term breaks had only increased my reluctance to leave the safety of the school compound. But in the second year, Wanjai persuaded me to accompany him and Leonard Mbũgua to Limuru.

Wanjai assured me that he and his friends had often walked the ten or fifteen miles and back on previous Nairobi Saturdays without any adverse effects. Besides, his father,

Reverend Jeremiah Gitau, had a car and would drive us back. Not that he, or I for that matter, had been in touch with anybody at home: it was always a matter of gamble, hope, and chance.

The first part of the trip went smoothly. We decided to visit my mother's place first and end up at his father's for the transport back. It turned out that my mother was in the fields near Limuru town, on a strip of land that had long been hers to cultivate, even before villagization. I had known the big Mugumo tree in its center since childhood. It symbolized a continuity in my life, and I felt like I was bringing the others to my *real* home. She fed us her famous potatoes roasted on an open fire.

Feeling good about ourselves, still sure that we had plenty of time, we decided, at Wanjai's insistence, to walk to Loreto Girls School just to see them in their flaming red uniforms. Wanjai and his friend wanted to confirm that the girls had hot showers, as the rumors claimed, instead of the cold ones we had at Alliance. After Loreto we would pass by Wanjai's home and then ride back to school, in style, in his father's car. So simple.

At Loreto we let the nun on duty at the office know that we had not come to visit anybody in particular, we just wanted to see the school. Uniformed Alliance boys coming just to visit? Not only did we get an escort to show us around, we were treated like stars, with the girls ogling us, some even whistling, strange in my ears, because I thought only boys did that. Unlike over a year ago, when I took my intermediate school exams at that location and all the girls seemed equally beautiful, this time I was able to tell some differences in their personalities, despite their red uniforms. Wanting to prolong the moment of adulation, we even accepted late afternoon tea with them, dismissing any suggestion that we might be late getting back by saying that we had a ride. When we finally left for Limuru, Wanjai stilled our worries: his father was certain to come to the rescue.

Well, he did not. Though he never raised his voice in anger, he was not amused and asked Wanjai why he brought his guests home so late in the day. In his calm preacher voice, he said that as we had not asked his permission to waste time, we must have had a plan to get back to Alliance, and we had better follow through with it. We were late back. The next Saturday we were confined to the school to cut grass as punishment. It was a lesson on how not to plan on the expectations of what others will do for you.

In time, and with each telling, the tale of our visit to Loreto became more dramatic, the inconveniences, fatigue, and dangers of walking alone in the dark morphing into a thrilling adventure. Wanjai must also have sung praises of my mother's art of roasting potatoes in the open because later many of his friends hinted that they would not mind going to Limuru with me on the next Nairobi Saturday. And was it really true that Loreto Girls School was not too far from where I lived? But since I could not count on somebody being at the new home, I always deflected the hints. I did not want to walk a guest the ten or fifteen miles and back on hungry stomachs. Besides, I could not conjure up another Loreto visit, which was obviously the main attraction.

24

In the second term, on another Nairobi Saturday, I broke my self-imposed restraint and invited Johana Mwalwala. Johana, a Mtaita, and I were classmates, he in B and I in A, but both residents in Dorm Two, Livingstone House. He was always polite and considerate, and this drew me to him. I confessed to him that I had no way of alerting home about the visit, that we were chancing it, and he understood. I think he just wanted to get away from the compound on a Nairobi Saturday.

We set out after breakfast, and by the early afternoon we could see Kamīrīthū. I was confident that if my mother was at home, she would find a way of feeding us her roasted potatoes at least. We would eat quickly, drink some porridge or tea, and walk back to school. This time there was no expectations of another person's car: we were going to rely on our feet. And there was no question of visiting Loreto or indulging in any other distraction. If we stayed within these parameters, everything would work out as hoped, and the nearer we got to Kamīrīthū, the more certain I was of a good outcome. But our plans never came to be.

Just before we reached the turn to my new home, we were caught up in a military dragnet. Armed black and white soldiers in camouflage, red berets, and green military vehicles and Land Rovers surrounded a huge crowd squatting in the sun in the plain below the village. I had hoped the Alliance uniform would make us invisible, but it didn't, and we were forced to join the captives. Mwalwala, being a Mtaita, was allowed to leave, but I had a long wait, weighed down by the anxiety I always carried: that my connection with a guerrilla fighter might keep me from returning to Alliance, ever. Every time I seemed to conquer that fear, other events would crop up to mock me with, Not so fast.

Eventually my turn came. I had learned my lessons from the past and answered all the questions about my brother and whether I knew his contacts, calmly pleading sincere ignorance to most of them, shielding myself behind being away at Alliance, a boarding school. Despite all my bravado about not letting fear rule me, I could not believe that this was happening to me on the only Saturday I had brought a visitor home by myself. Finally, they released me.

Wisely, Mwalwala had already headed back to school. I hurried home to tell my family what had happened, but they already knew. My mother said that it was really not necessary to come home before the end of the term. I grabbed whatever food there was and left. Shaken and disappointed, I walked back to school in the dark, alone. I was late, very late. I had committed the same offense twice. On Monday I was called to the principal's office.

25

I was sure that I was going to be caned, even expelled from the school. Since my admission, I had always wondered how long it would be before the fact of my brother being in the mountains caught up with me. Somehow, after that Churchill speech, I could not get rid of the image of Carey Francis as a defender of the British Empire. After all, he was an OBE. The image of the empire loyalist and the legend of the disciplinarian were in my mind as I entered the office.

He was in his eternal khaki wear. I stood before him, and his eyes pierced me the whole time. Why had I broken the school rule so badly that I had returned to school at midnight? This was the second time. Did I know how serious this breach of school rules was? Nairobi Saturday did not mean breaking rules. He appeared calm, but it seemed to me that he might, at any time, start stepping, rolling his tongue in his cheek, and fuming. I eyed the door and the windows.

I faced a dilemma. The whole of last Saturday lay before me. I could tell him about the raid, but did I have to talk about the questions and my responses? If I told him that my brother was out in the mountains fighting against Churchill's empire, I could be expelled from the sanctuary and have to return to the village and the community prison I had helped to build during my very first break as an Alliance student, the place that always reminded me of loss. Still, I decided to tell him everything.

There! At long last, my secret was out. I was relieved. It was my turn to dare him, silently, looking straight into his eyes, resigned to my fate. You are an officer of the British Empire. My brother is sworn to end the empire. Send me back to my mother, if you so wish, but I will never deny him. Not for you. Not for Alliance. My brother is a good man. All he ever asked for was the right to be free. Had your Churchill not fought Hitler so that his people would not be ruled by the Germans? You see, sir, my brother wants the same thing for his people. All he ever wanted was—Carey Francis cut off my flow of thoughts.

Had I been in my Alliance uniform last Saturday? he asked. It was the last thing I expected from his mouth. Alliance uniform? Of course, yes, with the badge and the logo, AHS, I said. He did not ask any more questions. You can go, but in future, be more careful. Some of those officers are scoundrels! he added, gritting his teeth.

I was completely taken aback, confused even, by his reaction. I was relieved and grateful that he did not dole out any punishment, but to call the British officers scoundrels? In the world of Carey Francis, politicians were either statesmen or scoundrels. Bureaucrats were either statesmen or scoundrels. Those who had detained me, even though white officers, were scoundrels for discounting the evidence of the Alliance uniform.

Only later did it hit me: he had not reacted to the fact that my brother was in the mountains. Or that my sister-in-law was in a maximum security prison. He did not even ask if I had taken the oath, which I had not. It was as if he knew my story all along. Or perhaps my story was not so unique, just one among many he had heard.

Indeed, I was to learn later that my case was not unique, that among my classmates were others who carried similar woes. In the early days of the state of emergency, the school, even during vacations, had become a sanctuary for victims of both sides of the conflict: those who feared retaliation by Mau Mau because their fathers were loyalist home guards, and those who feared retaliation by the colonial forces because their relatives were guerrillas in the mountains or captives in the concentration camps. The Franciscan reaction to my revelation put more cracks in my perception of a white monolith pitted against a black monolith, already challenged by the reality of many Africans, including some relatives, who fought on the colonial side. In a more personal way, his reaction went quite a long way to undercut the fear that had haunted my stay in the sanctuary, the fear that a discovery of my blood connection with the freedom fighters would somehow curtail my education.

One good attracts another, and I also got the welcome news soon afterward that Kĩambu Native African Location Council had awarded me a full scholarship. My arrears would be covered, and I would not have to pay tuition for the rest of my years at Alliance. My next holidays in August were the first that I would enjoy without the fear that money and politics would block my educational path. And then the unexpected happened.

26

I was about to return to school for the last term of my second year, when we learned that British forces had captured my brother. Since there was no official announcement, the news reached us through the grapevine from Banana Hills, where his in-laws lived. There were all sorts of rumors: he had been shot in the leg; no, in the head; no, the bullets had gone through the heart. One thing was constant: they had captured him alive. If true, that was a relief. Still, I feared that they would hang him at Gĩthũngũri the way they had many others before him. My fears were deepened by the fact that I did not know the circumstances of his capture.

Years later I would learn that Good Wallace and his men had fallen into an ambush soon after they themselves had ambushed a small convoy of British soldiers near Longonot. They managed to fight their way through the cordon and then ran in different directions. With more reinforcements, the enemy forces pursued them relentlessly, over hills and valleys, across rivers, day and night, through Gilgil, southern Nyandarwa. Some of his comrades fell to the enemy fire, but Good Wallace just managed to escape. He would tell a harrowing story of how at one time, completely exhausted, he fell down and crawled under a thick tea bush in the Brooke Bond Estate on the White Highlands side of Limuru, his gun beside him. The enemy soldiers were scattered all over the tea bushes, each following a different row, turning over the thickets with their rifles. At one point, a soldier was literally standing above my brother's hiding place. Good Wallace thought he had met his fate and opened his mouth to beg for his life, *hapana ua*, don't kill, but as in a nightmare, no voice came out. It was just as well. Soon the enemy went away, still searching among the bushes.

Good Wallace spent the next couple of days trying to reconnect with his remaining comrades, in vain. Alone, with the gun as his only companion, he assessed his situation: he had once escaped into the forests under a hail of police bullets; now he had escaped death by the luckiest whim. Should he tempt fate again? The choice was between accepting a heroic death or giving up for the hope of fighting another day.

He chose the latter. Burying his gun under a Mugumo tree, he crossed rivers and walked through forest slopes and coffee plantations all the way to Chief Karūga's family homestead, near Banana Hills, quite a distance. Good Wallace knew the family in the days when my sister Gathoni was their neighbor in Kīambaa.

It was very early in the morning when he appeared at the door and identified himself to Grace Nduta, Karūga's wife, who welcomed him and made a meal for him, the first homemade food he had eaten in years. She was the one who quietly broke the news to her husband. Chief Charles Karūga Koinange ensured that my brother did not fall into vengeful hands. We did not know what tale the chief told, but it was a relief when we learned that Good Wallace had been taken to Manyani concentration camp. He would live, at least.

The nationalist guerrillas were being hit hard. On October 21, 1956, the British forces captured Dedan Kīmathi, the Mau Mau guerrilla leader, the one they feared most, the stuff of legends. The image of the wounded warrior chained to his hospital bed would haunt me for a long time, clashing as it did with that of the legendary Kīmathi whom Ngandi told me of in his stories. I wondered what Ngandi, wherever he now resided, would say about the loss of Kĩmathi. No doubt he would claim that they had merely captured his shadow, that the real Kĩmathi still roamed the Nyandarwa Hills and slopes of Mount Kenya, vowing to fight to the end, proclaiming that it was better to die fighting for freedom than to live on bended knees.

Still, the capture of Dedan Kĩmathi, following that of my brother, left a sense of defeat in the air and an emptiness in me. But there were signs within Kenya and the world that the challenge to the imperial order that Kĩmathi symbolized was being enacted elsewhere in Africa.

27

A few months before Kĩmathi's capture, on July 26, 1956, Egypt's Colonel Gamal Abdel Nasser, who had seized power in 1952, the same year as the start of the Mau Mau War in Kenya, announced the nationalization of the Suez Canal to provide funding for the construction of the Aswan High Dam. It seemed to me that Nasser had suddenly made Africa a player in world politics, with leaders from Eisenhower to Khrushchev to Mao all paying close attention. The Nasserite act had clearly angered the British and French stockholders in the Suez Canal Company, and the shock waves reached us even at Alliance.

Carey Francis called an emergency school assembly, during which he described Nasser as a scoundrel and the nationalization a robbery, explaining the history of the canal from its construction by Ferdinand de Lesseps in 1868 to its eventual ownership by the British Suez Canal Company. The history was new to me, but it seemed obvious that a canal that had been dug out of Egyptian territory belonged to Egypt, just as the lands occupied by British settlers clearly belonged to Kenya. France might have provided the engineering expertise and Britain the capital, but what about the Egyptian land and labor?

Carey Francis was passionately against nationalization. But when, on October 29 of that same year, Israel, France, and Britain invaded Egypt to retake control of the canal, he thought it a mistake and told us so, arguing that two wrongs did not make a right. Carey Francis never ceased to amaze.

28

Mirroring all of this political upheaval was my own spiritual upheaval, the pivotal moment of which came toward the end of August, during my second year. David Martin had organized a special Christian Union event for an evangelist to show and discuss a Billy Graham film, *Souls in Conflict*. The guest evangelist himself was associated with the Billy Graham crusades. The meeting, which took place in the dining hall, was open to everybody, and there was good attendance. After the film, the evangelist said a few words.

It was evening. Standing on the same stage that had witnessed conjuring tricks, debates, Shakespeare, and counter-Shakespeare, the evangelist began by quoting the Bible,

Romans 3:23: *For we have all sinned and come short of the glory of God.* He slowly looked at us, in such a way that I felt as if he were pointing at me in particular, then went straight to the heart of the listener, creating a vivid vision of the fire that awaited sinners in Hell. And they deserved it, we deserved it, and no good works or learning or books would save us from it. He was masterful, talking to everybody and yet aiming every word at me, or so it seemed. And yet he and I were complete strangers. This God terrified me. I don't want to go to Hell, I felt myself saying, surprised because I had heard the same words many times before, and they had never had that kind of effect on me. But Hell was not inevitable, he now said, creating another vision of salvation. The God of wrath and vengeance had become the God of infinite mercy and love. John bore witness to this in 3:16: *For God so loved the world that he gave his only begotten son, that whosoever believeth in him should not perish but have everlasting life. For God sent not his son into the world to condemn the world but that the world through him might be saved.*

He continued talking as if he and God knew each other intimately. God did not force humans to choose one way or another. He gave us freedom of choice, free will. You can choose Heaven or Hell, he said, again looking and pointing at me. Even when I tried to hide behind others, he still found me with his eyes and finger. I believed in freedom of choice. He was appealing to my better nature, my reason, to accept unreason by faith alone. And then, on behalf of God, he gave me an offer taken straight out of the book of Revelation 3:20: *Behold I stand at the door and knock; if any man hear my voice, and open the door; I will come in to him and sup with him and he with me.*

I did not have to go anywhere or do anything dramatic: just open the door. He made it even easier for me. He told us to close our eyes that we might appeal to God for strength and guidance. My eyes still closed, I heard him speak directly to God, asking him to help me make the right choice. Me, yes me, for it seemed he directed his voice at me the whole time. God is not going to rush to the door and open it for you by force. You have to let him in. Will you? He told us, me, not to answer by voice. If I made a choice, would I please raise my hand, without opening my eyes? Yes, it really felt he was appealing to me. I felt my heart breaking into pieces. Something was giving way, a surrender of the will, thought, and reason. I could visualize his eyes on me, watching to see if I would raise my hand in total surrender and submission. I did, not caring if any other person had also done so. After all, he had been speaking to me alone.

You have made the biggest decision of your life. He talked a little bit more, and then told me to lower my hand and open my eyes. There was silence. David Martin said that people were free to leave but asked anybody who had raised their hands and accepted Jesus as their personal savior to please remain behind, together with those who had already done so before. There was indeed a small group who had always claimed to know Jesus more intimately than the rest of us. I stayed behind, sure that I would be the only one. The majority left, glancing behind to see who had been snared.

I was one of the snared but relieved that I was not alone. We were a large group of new converts, welcomed by the earlier converts into the fold. We had been elevated to their spiritual plane. Most prominent among them was Elijah Kahonoki*, or E.K., who had always worn his faith on his sleeve. The evangelist spoke with triumph but warned us that there would be many temptations in the way. If Satan had been shameless enough to tempt Jesus, who were we to think that the devil would leave us alone? But we could take strength from His triumph. E.K. assured us that the Christian fellowship of the saved would always be with us in our fights with the tempter.

Evangelism was not new to Alliance. By 1949, the Balokole, adherents of the Jesus-is-my-personal-savior movement, which had originated in Rwanda, had arrived in Kenya. Some Alliance boys became adherents and passed on the tradition. Although they were faithful members of the Christian Union that met regularly to study scriptures, the Balokole, or Saved, had their own separate group and held additional prayer meetings.

Carey Francis, for all his sermons about the House of the Interpreter, was not involved in the spiritual enterprise of the breast-beating, Jesus-is-my-personal-savior type of worship. Christianity for him was like a long-distance race, and he often talked of pacing oneself so that at the end one might say: I have fought the good fight, I have completed the race, I have kept the faith. For him, acts and conduct that proclaimed faith were more important than words that

* Not his real name.

Christian Union with visitors from outside the school, 1956: Edward Carey Francis (second row, second from left); Ngũgĩ (second row, fourth from left); Joshua Omange (second row, fifth from left); David Martin, master in charge of Christian Union (second row, middle). In the background is the Alliance High School chapel.

shouted belief. But he did not disparage evangelism, probably seeing its value: the Balokole were the most faithful leaders of Sunday schools, walking many miles every Sunday to reach those farthest removed from Alliance.

29

In time, quite a few of those who had raised their hands and remained behind with us gradually slid into their old ways. But my classmate Joseph Omange, E.K., and I formed a three-person cabal and built a spiritual fortress around ourselves. We three were determined not to let Satan into our midst. We met early in the chapel every day, read the Bible, and prayed, before the main congregation arrived. E.K., having accepted Jesus as his personal savior long before we had, was leader of our trio. Over the years he had made good connections with the evangelical community in the villages around and beyond, in Nairobi and other cities. Through him we felt connected to this larger community of the Balokole outside the walls of Alliance.

One of the most important responsibilities of the Saved was bearing witness to our Lord's infinite grace and mercy, so as to convert others to the way of the Cross. E.K. did this effortlessly, while I was tongue-tied most times. I found it difficult to meet with complete strangers and start telling them about my faith. It felt like bragging and putting others on the defensive. It seemed so intrusive. But that was the point, E.K. told me: the idea was to make the sinner uncomfortable and become aware of the Satan comfortably snuggled in his heart.

The other ritual in the circles in which E.K. moved was confessing one's sins to the band of the Saved. Each speaker, as moved, would tell how he or she had first found the Lord. As if borrowing from the *Confessions of Saint Augustine*, one dramatized the depth of one's depravity in the previous existence, before the Lord had felt pity and showed him or her the way of the Cross. Often the confessors recounted multiple encounters with the devil since conversion, to show how relentless Satan was in the attempt to dislodge them from their embrace of the Cross. Some were very creative in their graphic descriptions of the temptations they had faced. A few had managed to beat the tempter, but others had fallen, and they attracted the most intense prayers of support in their fight against Satan. The bigger the temptation, whether one succumbed to it or not, the more the tempted grew in stature. Sins of sexual desire drew the most attention. No sin seemed bigger. After all, sex was the original sin that had made all humans come short of the glory of God. Some narrators went into titillating details that made one leave the group with more sexual images in mind than before.

When my turn came, I found, to my dismay, that I had no sins to confess. And yet I must have sinned! Everybody sinned! If we said that we had no sins, we were deceiving ourselves. Omange had the same problem as me: a sinner who did not know his sins. We could only come up with trivial ones like anger, rude words, or cheating by reading for an extra hour when we were required to be in bed by nine. But E.K. always had plenty of sins to confess, especially harboring desires for the opposite sex. On each occasion, he had managed to eke out a victory against Satan.

Omange and I looked like imposters. In the end, we drifted away from groups outside the school but retained our cabal and our daily routine of additional prayers and Bible reading. E.K. never tired of keeping us informed about his meetings with our other brothers and sisters in Christ. We trusted E.K., who would clear our doubts with biblical quotations. He spoke with the authority of one who had conversed directly with God, which always deepened my doubts about my own state: I could never be sure that God had spoken directly to me.

Once I asked him about the language in which God spoke to him. English, he said. And how could one tell the difference between God and Jesus when they spoke to him? Was there a difference in the quality and volume of the two voices? Jesus and God were one and the same. I must keep the faith, and I would soon be able to tell the difference. Such questions, so important because they genuinely troubled me, started creating tension between us.

One of the most contentious came over the color of God and Jesus. On September 26, 1956, Sam Ntiro, then lecturer at the Makerere Art School, and his student, Elimo Njau,* had visited our school to talk to us about art and show us paintings of a black Christ, pointing out that Jesus was not born in white Europe. Although they had no paintings of God, they argued that He revealed Himself in the different colors of different cultures. God after all made man in his image, to black people in his splendid blackness and to white people in his silvery whiteness.

There were many skeptics. All the pictures that we had seen in books and magazines were of a white, blue-eyed Jesus. Some of the white teachers told us that it was not necessary to see God through racial lenses. God had no color. Jesus was white, and white was not a color. E.K. took the same view of a colorless God and Jesus but could not explain why all the pictures in Christian literature had both

---

* Years later, Elimo Njau would become one of the leading artists in Africa; he founded the famous Paa ya Paa art gallery, still active today.

deities as white. I was on Ntiro and Njau's side: if God made man in his image, then blackness was equally a color of God. Each of us could know how God looked by looking at ourselves.

I was troubled by my inability to hear the voice of God or lead new followers to the Cross, the way E.K. did. I came up with a plan: if I could convert one person, if I could somehow bring one soul to Christ, I would have my doubts stilled. I started telling people about my faith, mostly select friends on a one-to-one basis. But the few times I tried, people would look at me and laugh, or ask questions for which I had no real answers. My friends were the worst, for they said outright that they did not believe me. Or some would playfully ask me to confess my sins to them so that they could compare theirs to mine. They had not seen me breast-beating and shouting *tukutendereza* in a mass meeting. I told E.K. about my problems, that my appeals to reason always elicited more arguments than conversions. No, you have to appeal to the heart, not the mind, he told me. Faith was not a matter of logic. He told me not to worry, that it took time to master ways of dislodging Satan from the souls of the fallen. But I was disappointed that my attempts to convert never bore a single fruit. E.K., on the other hand, reported many victories: he had a small following of those who claimed that it was through him that they had found the Lord.

One morning, in our last year, we met as usual. E.K. had specifically requested the meeting. After our rituals of prayers and daily diet of scriptures, he said he had something to tell us about the temptation of the flesh. We were about to pray for him to be stronger next time, when he told us that it was more than that. He had put a sister-in-Christ in the family way. It was a great sin, bigger than any that he had confessed to before. It shocked us, but it also made us feel the bigness of his commitment: he had confessed, and he was now humbly asking us to pray for him. After the prayers, Omange spoke frankly and sincerely. What was done was done. We would continue supporting him. For a start, we pledged to be at his side at the wedding, which we assumed would be quite soon so that the child would be born in wedlock. E.K. hesitated. He was not planning to marry her, and no amount of pleading would make him change his mind. Omange burst into tears. We felt betrayed.

Later, I learned that those temptations that E.K. used to confess to were real, and the lady he told us about was not the first that he had put in the family way. Somehow his heart-wrenching confessions kept him a trusted member of the evangelical community. But Omange and I could not recover from the shock of his categorical refusal to marry the woman. Our cabal disintegrated. We never met again as the evangelical trio, although Omange and I retained our Christian fellowship, now deepened by our experience of betrayal.

It made me recall with renewed curiosity the Franciscan view of Christian life as being more than mere expressions of piety, that it had to show itself in everyday acts and choices; in the classroom, in voluntary work, in games. Temptations to the will could come during any of these activities and not necessarily in a dramatic encounter with Satan alone in the mountains and on desert plains. The fall of our cabal left a hole in my heart and increased my doubts. But I never gave up in my attempts to convert the souls of the people I knew, despite the mounting failures.

30

My religious fervor, however strong, could not dim my passionate enthusiasm for theater. A Shakespearean production of *Henry IV, Part I* signaled the end of the school year, and I auditioned for a part. I did not land a speaking role, but I was one of the foot soldiers, holding wooden spikes the whole time, part of the silent human background. Being a participant, though mute, inhibited my imagination from meandering and creating additions to the universe unfolding, for I had to keep focused, but the struggle for power and the violence that went with it was clearer in this historical drama than it had been in *As You Like It*.

During the production, I became fascinated by the progression of the actors from their initial imperfection to their near flawless execution on the final performance. I came to value the character of theater as a collective effort: the behind-the-scenes mutual dependence of the minor and the major players; the prop, costume, and light management; and the directing to create an enjoyable spectacle before a cheering audience. Nobody who saw the flawless performance would have known how often, during the rehearsals, the actors forgot their lines and positions, or the many ten-

Ngũgĩ in Alliance High School's 1956 performance of Shakespeare's
Henry IV, Part I (bottom row, first from left)

sions and clashes of egos that would bring the preparations
to a halt. The collective success was intoxicating and more
than made up for the constant threat of chaos. Even the
drop in adrenaline on the days that followed the last curtain
could not dim the joyful memory of common struggle.

But outside the joy and travails of participation, the
political theater onstage was mimicking the real theater of
politics outside the school gates. In the world, the Soviets
had invaded Hungary, an event that elicited condemnation

from Carey Francis, and in the country, the war between the Mau Mau and the British was still going on. All three theaters affected me in different ways. The one on the stage entertained my mind, and the one in Hungary raised my curiosity, but the one in the country threatened my body. The fact that Good Wallace was no longer an active guerrilla but a prisoner of war did not prevent anxieties from hovering over my return to Kamĩrĩthũ at the end of the year. I left the sanctuary in December, the end of my second year, looking forward to a safe return to its bosom in January, for my third year.

31

My mother remained of few words even in the hardest of times. She was always happy to see me and to hear of my progress in school, but she felt surer of my safety at school than at our new home and was relieved when the vacation ended. I would have liked to hear her talk more about her thoughts and feelings about what was unfolding, the arrest and detention of my brother, for instance, or the interrogations she had undergone. But to her, everything was in the hands of God, and her proverb, *Gũtirĩ ũtukũ ũtakĩa*, every night ends with dawn, summed up her view of the world.

Her love of soil was deep; she was at her happiest when working in the fields, turning the soil over, nursing the crops, and harvesting the produce of her hands. I could see that she appreciated the fact that I was not afraid of working the land, that the high school experience had not softened my hands. She never said, you must go to the fields today, but would say, I'll roast potatoes for you in the field, an offer she knew I would not refuse.

She was an early riser, and she was not always sure that we would follow her, but she made sure to let us know where she would be. One time, rather late in the morning, my younger brother and I joined her at her favorite spot. She clearly had not been expecting us, but she was pleased to see us armed with our usual tools of hoes and machetes. At midday she made a fire near the Mugumo tree and selected the best potatoes for roasting. She always roasted many more than she knew we could finish, in keeping with her long-held philosophy that an unexpected visitor might pass by. And that day he did. It was my father, who, hidden from view by the tree, seemed to appear from nowhere. I had not seen my father since the day I said farewell to him in the old homestead before I left for Alliance. Now he and his other wives were in a different section of the village, and I had not been to visit them the last five vacations. My mother did not seem surprised to see him, and I assumed that this was not the first time he had visited her in the fields.

She asked him to sit down, saying he was in time for a share of roasted potatoes. He asked how I was doing in school, remonstrated with me for not having been to see him, but quickly showered blessings to show he harbored no ill will. Otherwise there was not much conversation between us, or between him and my mother. As we ate together in the field under the shadow of the Mugumo tree, I could not help but wonder whether it was in such a field, or this very one, that he had wooed her. After our luncheon, my father went on his way.

My younger brother, who had never had the same kind of reconciliation with him that I once had, did not look on the visit generously: I'm sure he turns up only when he's hungry. My mother was prompt in her censure. He is still your father. Don't you judge him. Let him judge himself. To smooth the awkward moment, I asked my mother about the story she had once told us of how they had found each other. She just smiled and ignored my request. But my question, or the visit, must have mellowed her, for suddenly she started talking, with uncharacteristic openness, about not him but the tree. She believed it was sacred and healing. For some reason, she made us look at its roots carefully. They were strong and deep, and that's why a Mugumo never succumbed to prevailing winds and changing weather and lasted many years. Do you know that this particular one has been here since before the coming of the colonizer, even before your great-great-great-grandparents? When we asked her playfully how she knew its age, she said it was time to resume work. But then she answered: Because people have lived here longer than the tree and they tell the story and they pass on the story and we add to the story.

I had never told her about my spiritual strivings, but she might have detected a restlessness in me, and the story might have been her way of touching on it. Many years later my writing would start with a short story titled *Mugumo, the Fig Tree*.

1957

*A Tale of the Street
and the Chamber*

32

The Alliance that I returned to on January 17, 1957, was no longer a sanctuary in my mind. But although its lure as a refuge was fading, it retained, and even increased, its character as a window through which I could catch glimpses of what was unfolding outside, in the country and in the world, and as a filter through which I could sort out the meaning of what I saw. These roles of window and filter came through the editorial frames of the school assembly, the classrooms, and the *Saturday Evening Paper.*

SEP was founded in 1943 to fill the vacuum left by the suspension of the official school magazine due to wartime shortages of printing paper. The student editors of *SEP* wrote everything by hand and read it to the assembly. By the time the official magazine resumed, after the war, *SEP* had become a fixture in the weekly calendar.

I'll always remember my first experience of *SEP.* We had gathered in the dining hall after dinner, eagerly awaiting the famed Saturday entertainments to start, when the school captain, Manasseh Kegode, stood on the raised platform at the end of the hall and called the audience to order to hear the news broadcast in Caesar's Kingdom, which was

greeted with applause by those who knew that the kingdom in reference was Alliance. Then a student, one of the
two current editors, stood at the platform with a file in his
hands and read out: *Saturday Evening Paper;* Founders:
M. E. Mugwanja and B. M. Gecaga. That, as I later found
out, was the unfailing preliminary ritual of the newscast.

The paper's quality depended on the editors' selec-
tion of material, their writing and reading abilities, and
their own body language of diffidence or confidence. The
1957 team of Allan Ngũgĩ and Lucas Ritho infused *SEP*
with a certain dignity and authority. In 1958 my classmates
George Ong'ute and Joab Onyango sustained the high level
of clarity in oral delivery and maintained the grand tradition of the variety of material offered, the judicious balance
of trivia and gravitas.

The trivia ranged from mostly satirical stories of events
on the campus to some regular, popular columns, like one
that took the logic of English spelling and grammar to
absurd limits. If the adjectives *tall* and *long* were conjugated
as *tall, taller,* and *tallest; long, longer, longest;* why couldn't
good become *gooder, goodest;* and *bad, badder, baddest*? If the
past tense of *go* was *went,* why couldn't that of *do,* almost
identical in spelling, become *dwent*? Others made fun of
English pronunciation as impacted by the African languages
of our different origins. Fairly constant in the trivia were
humorous takes on boys, their names withheld of course,
who might have been spotted dating girls in the valley; or
censorious but humorous anecdotes about the newcomers,
who had been sighted exhibiting such unbecoming behav-

iors as spitting on the ground, or swallowing their morning porridge noisily. But there could also be serious stories of adventures and misadventures outside the premises of the school, particularly during excursions to the big city.

The gravitas, my favorite, were the territorial and international stories, culled from the *East African Standard*. My interest in outside events as they affected Kenya had started with Ngandi, and I still looked at any news through the worldview that had evolved from my conversations with him, generally sympathetic to nationalist sentiments. In its own way, *SEP* could somehow capture, to my satisfaction at least, the prevailing mood in the country and the world. Such was the case in its coverage of the Suez Canal conflict.

33

The struggle over Suez had left a feeling that something, a change, was afoot in the world. In Britain, the crisis, or rather the failure of the tripartite mission, had forced a change of leadership. On January 9, 1957, Anthony Eden resigned as British prime minister and was replaced by Harold Macmillan. Within three months Macmillan was welcoming one of the most dramatic events that would redraw the power map of Africa and her relationship to the world. Ghana's independence from Britain on March 6, 1957, eclipsed that of Libya, wrested from Italy in December 1951; Tunisia and Morocco, both wrested from the French in 1956; and even that of Sudan, from Britain, also in 1956.

Despite their number, we were hardly aware of those other, earlier independences. Ghana's success, however, was duly noted in *SEP*, capturing our imaginations as no other recent event in Africa had.

It could not be lost on me that the first-ever direct election of African members to the Legislative Council, the Kenya Colony law-making body, known by the acronym Legco, took place on March 10, four days after Ghana's independence. The election, despite the exclusion of Central Province and the fact that Africans were overwhelmingly outnumbered by the European and Asian elected members, was historic. Three days later the eight members formed the African Elected Members Organization, AEMO, and rejected as null and void the Lyttelton Plan under which they had been elected. The phrase *null and void* entered our student vocabulary immediately.

It emerged slowly, but Kĩmathi's capture in 1956 and hanging in February 1957 marked the beginning of a crucial shift of political theater from the mountains to the Nairobi streets and the imperial chambers in London. In pre–Mau Mau days, the street was a popular base from which to openly challenge imperial chambers, but the state of emergency declared in 1952 had literally outlawed the street as a theater of social and political action. After the 1957 elections, however, the street resumed the role it had played earlier, once again becoming a living stage on which unfolded the drama of unexpected scenes and actors.

In my mind, political actors had always appeared as fictional characters. In the Ngandi period of my youth, the pre–Mau Mau nationalist lineup had loomed larger than life. Their struggles against the giant white ogre from across the sea were epic battles fought with fiery swords that lit up the dark. Sometimes I saw the heroes battling it out in the shadows with the charging feet of wild rhinos and the roar of lions. Now, confined as they were to exile, prisons, and concentration camps, the characters had faded in outline, but didn't epic heroes always end up chained between rocks of ages or locked up in dungeons-within-dungeons?

The new post-Ngandi, post–Mau Mau nationalist characters seemed life size, actors on a stage I could comprehend. Perhaps this was because we were witnesses to their entrances and sometimes their exits, or because of their distinct disadvantage of having been forbidden to form political parties based on an area larger than a district. The Africans used ingenuity to overcome this circumscription and local confinement by grouping themselves under the umbrella of African Elected Members Organization, AEMO. Still, it remained a case of too many bulls in one kraal. I did not yearn to catch a glimpse of them with the intensity I had shown for the older actors. But their clashes with their settler adversaries and their shifting alliances with their Indian counterparts fueled the excitement of the present drama. Sometimes they would move their act from the streets of Nairobi to those of London to confront the imperial throne, but they would always come back to Kenya to report to the masses that thronged the streets, becoming instant poets, their speeches poetry. The peaceful, fun-loving, and singing throng from the slums made the dwellers of the exclusive suburbs tremble with terror of the unknown and shut themselves inside their palaces within reach of guns and telephones.

Tom Mboya's confrontation with Michael Blundell, the settler leader, in their Legislative Council debates, created sparks that always seemed on the verge of lighting the prairie on fire, but the sparks were contained in the polite chambers of the legislature, following the tradition of the British Parliament. These gentlemen, always in suits except for the occasional nod to African dress, demanded power, unlike the long-haired, armed guerrillas in their hodgepodge of dirty rags, animal skins, and torn boots, who threatened to seize power, smashing open the walls that chained the epic heroes of yesteryear.

We at Alliance could not take our gaze away from the drama in the streets. Each day brought out something new that impacted our view of the country, the continent, and the world. Our activities on the school compound now played out against the background of the all-year political theater in the streets. At times the compound and the street would come face to face. I felt this interaction profoundly at a scouting event.

34

The scout camp, like the chapel, the playing field, and the classroom, sought to instill in students the ideal of service. Scouting was voluntary, but it had all the exciting elements of physical and mental discipline, loyalty, fellowship, and obedience to authority, a kind of secular religion without the rites of a particular spiritual order. As my mother would point out with horror, the word *scout* in Gĩkũyũ sounded like *thika hiti*,* a professional burier of dead hyenas, a possibility that always made me wary of the movement. But in 1955 I watched with admiration as the troops came back from camping with stories of adventures in the wild that exhibited their knowledge of outdoor life. Their badges, covering their shirtsleeves, shirt pockets, and shoulders, and their colorful scarves, were irresistibly attractive. The scouts managed the canteen, a very well-run business where one could buy buttered slices of bread. Many of the masters were involved in scouting activities. Even Carey Francis, though not active in the school's troops, had been a scout-master in Cambridge.

But given its colorful presence at Alliance, it was easy to forget that the movement was born during the defense of the British Empire in Africa. Scouting started in Kenya in 1910, three years after Lord Baden-Powell founded the movement at Brownsea, near Dorset, in England. Initially it was confined to Europeans and Indians, but the first African troop was officially recognized by the HQ in Nairobi in 1929.

I joined the scout movement in 1956 and vowed to do my best to fulfill my duty to God and queen, help other people at all times, and obey the scout law. I learned that

* See *Dreams in a Time of War.*

Scouts: James Mathenge (on left) and Ngũgĩ (on right)

a scout was loyal; useful and helpful to others; brother to every other scout; courteous; a friend to all, including animals; and was thrifty and clean in thought, word, and deed. He smiled and whistled under all difficulties and obeyed orders of authority without question. A scout's honor was to be trusted. Although the bit about the queen was difficult to swallow, the promises were not at odds with Alliance, my religious fellowship, or my upbringing. Values of frugality, doing the maximum with the minimum, and not despairing in difficult situations but trying to figure a way out appealed to me. Among the many skills of survival we learned, knots occupied an important place. I knew some of them by their Gĩkũyũ names, but in English, names like *bowline, square knot,* and *sheet bend* made the knots sound extraordinarily difficult to master. Ironically, this helped me to not take my knowledge for granted or think that I knew all the knots there were to know.

Aside from being instructive, scouting was fun. I enjoyed camping at Rowallan in Nairobi, making trips to Ngong Hills for a magnificent view of the Great Rift Valley, and journeying to Hell's Gate for the incredible sight of hot steam springing from the bowels of the earth. In October 1956 Princess Margaret visited Kenya, which led to a particularly memorable scouting experience. I was among a party of fifty boys and twenty scouts who went to Nairobi to line the streets, waving small Union Jacks as the slow-moving motorcade wound its way around the stadium. As scouts, we were better positioned to get a glimpse of the passing princess. But it was the milling crowd of children waving the flag that left the biggest impression.

35

My most memorable scouting experience, however, was the 1957 jamboree at the graveyard of Lord Baden-Powell for the centennial celebration of his birth. Accompanied by three teachers, Omondi, Ogutu, and Smith, as well as Mrs. Smith, twenty-four scouts left at seven a.m. on Friday,

Ngũgĩ (on right) with Johana Mwalwala (on left) hiking in
Ngong Hills, 1956. Below is the Great Rift Valley.

Ngũgĩ at Hell's Gate, Naivasha, 1956. Behind are the natural hot springs.

February 22, in the school truck. Past Nairobi, every new name of place—Ruiru, Juja, Mang'u, Thika—sounded magical. At the Blue Post Hotel we crossed the bridge over the Chania. It was the biggest river I had ever seen in my life. Even more breathtaking was the roaring waterfall to our right, but this was only the beginning of the wonders. As we drove through Murang'a, then Fort Hall, I was held captive by the landscape of ridges and deep valleys that lay together in parallel. On the slopes, one could spot people walking two or three cows along dusty paths to find grass, while others worked in the fields of corn.

We zigzagged up and down the slopes, ridge to ridge, till we reached a small plain along which meandered the Thagana River, said to originate from Mount Kenya to join other streams to become the Tana River, which flows all the way to the coast and the Indian Ocean. Thereafter it was another climb toward Karatina, famous for its wartime agriculture that aided the British war economy but where, after the war, the advanced processing plants were razed to the ground to prevent Africans from competing with white settlers. One or two miles later we were in Nyeri town, then the capital of Central Province. I had always been drawn to thick forests, rugged rocks, and other natural sculptures, but the landscape between Murang'a and Nyeri left a lasting impression, years later to appear as the fictional landscape in my first novel, *The River Between*. The images that would later launch my novel-writing efforts were thus formed on my way to honor Baden-Powell.

In the afternoon, we took part in what was dubbed an

Asante rally, a thank-you affair to the memory of Baden-Powell, an incredible assembly of boys of all races from all parts of the country and the world. The sheer magnitude of the crowd of secular worshippers of this iconic figure was itself a sight to cherish, remember, and reflect upon, a vision of peace and cooperation across races dreamed up amid the carnage of another colonial war.

For me, Nyeri was not about Baden-Powell alone; in my heart, it was also about the native-born Dedan Kĩmathi and

Kenya Scouts Jamboree at Nyeri Showground, 1957:
Ngũgĩ (on left); Kenneth Mbũgua (on right) at the
February 23 Asante rally in honor of Baden-Powell

Stanley Mathenge and the other larger-than-life guerrillas from Nyeri who were coping with survival in a real forest, unlike those of us who were choosing to learn survival skills only to affirm our loyalty to God, queen, and colonial authority.

Once, trying to push my way through the milling crowd without losing sight of the Alliance contingent, I bumped into Kenneth Mbũgua, my Limuru childhood friend. What a coincidence! We spent some time together and even posed for pictures, our scout's knives hanging from our belts. We discussed everything, from our experiences in scouting to books we had read. It was always a treat to argue with Kenneth about books, for it stretched the limits of our understanding in the frantic search for reinforcements to buttress our side of the argument.

It was inevitable that Kenneth and I would resume our eternal dispute about the license to write. This time I was not as aggressive in my rejoinders, curious about the progress of his own book. He appreciated the comments I had made about simple sentences and the virtues of the Anglo-Saxon word. Goodwill established, I tried to press my advantage toward, well, my first convert. I knew his obstinacy too well to approach the subject directly. I had to be circumspect as I slipped into my Jesus-is-my-personal-savior mode, still trying to snag my first catch. He could learn from the Bible, I told him, more than simple words of its language. But Kenneth proved skeptical and did not fall for my sly attempts to move from English language structure to soul restructuring. His soul remained stuck to his sinful body the way his characters remained stuck in the city, probably victims of police raids and their own sins.

Eventually our talk drifted from books and salvation, about which we never seemed to agree, to life in the new village. We were struck by the fact that, living in the same congested village, we hardly ever met the way we used to in the old homestead. Ever since the loss of the old homestead, I had been haunted by the melancholy of the new. We lived in the same village, but we were a collection of strangers, lonely villagers. It may have arisen from my yearning for something, anything to make me feel at home in the new, but increasingly I found myself troubled by the lack of any social activity that could bring the youth of the new village together. Kenneth expressed the same feeling. Maybe we who had had the benefit of a high school education and teacher training could lead the way and contribute something to help the community discover its soul. Kenneth seemed to warm to the idea of contributing to a community spirit more than he had to that of rescuing his own.

36

The challenge of forging a togetherness among the youth of the new villages would not leave my mind. When later I went back to Kamĩrĩthũ on April 18 for the first break of the year, I started contacting Limuru boys and girls now in high school, and those in the last years of their primary, to explore ways in which we might work together. This took me to many homes in the different parts of Kamĩrĩthũ and in neighboring villages. I began to connect with the different families of the old homestead while also discovering and making contact with new families. Instead of the melancholy I had seen reflected in the canopy of smoke over the village, I began to see the buoyant spirit of youth rising, expressing itself in many little things: walks in the narrow streets; informal gatherings in corners; occasional dancing in people's homes.

I returned to Alliance for the second term, a little bit more at ease with the new village. On the next Nairobi Saturday, I invited Allan Ngũgĩ, the famous editor of *SEP*, to come home with me, and he loved the novelty and the challenge of walking ten miles on foot. We found my mother at home. She roasted some potatoes for us, and afterward Allan confided that they were some of the best he had ever eaten. His appreciation was like an embrace of one of the most constant images in my life. My mother's roast had come to symbolize continuity despite the many changes in my life. Her last roast at the foot of the Mugumo tree and the talk that ensued about adding on to a story would be imprinted in my mind for years to come; it had already affected my attitude toward the village.

There was not a single mishap, the first time on a return to the village that a calamity had not befallen me. On our way back, I could appreciate the joy of walking and talking, without a memory of terror or anxiety of being late to school. It was amid our talk of different futures, immersed in many topics, that an idea of how best to carry out the

Baden-Powell spirit in Kamĩrĩthũ stole into my consciousness: instead of a scout troop, why not a debating club,
where the youth of the village would receive and add to the
story?

37

The debating society at Alliance was one of the oldest student clubs, started in 1939. The first motion, *Should Germany's colonial claims be accepted by Britain?* was an ironic case
of the colonized debating the merits of rival imperialisms
and presumably taking sides. But this started a tradition of
the society tackling political themes. Good debaters were
instant heroes, especially when it came to interschool contests. Such was the case involving the fourth-year Kĩmani
Nyoike and his Kagumo counterpart, Paul Mwema. I was
in my first year, part of the crowd that went to witness two
obstinate giants go at each other with relentless verbal
onslaughts, vying for our attention and allegiance. They
talked without notes, fluently. Where did people get the
courage to stand before such a crowd and air their views? I
would ask myself, time and again, mesmerized.

When finally, on another occasion, I contributed to
a debate, the question of courage did not arise. *Western
Education has done more harm than good in Africa* was the
motion. As the proponents and opponents continued, I felt
that frivolity was winning out over the seriousness the subject demanded. I recalled all the talks I used to have with

Ngandi about education, land, and religion. I raised my hand. As the debates were then mostly dominated by third and fourth years, the intervention of a first year raised eyebrows and curiosity. I did not have the eloquence of words and smoothness in delivery, but I had the clarity of passion. I held a pencil in the air. All eyes were fixed on it. I told a story. A person comes to your house. He takes your land. In exchange he gives you a pencil. Is this fair exchange? I would rather he kept his pencil and I kept my land. It was a huge effort. I sat down, breathless. The applause that followed told me the analogy had worked. It might even have helped swing the debate in favor of the motion. Of course, the contradiction was clear: all of us, for and against the motion, were at Alliance in pursuit of the Western education we had censured. But I learned the power of images in clarifying complex relations. Additionally, my intervention made an impression on the leadership of the debating society.

I became an avid participant in debates, if without that same kind of impact. Over the years, however, a few others and I became increasingly critical of the format. I felt that too many in the audience were passive; something was missing. When I became part of the leadership of the debating society, we discussed how we could inject drama into the sessions. I wanted consistent fire, or at least sparks, and it could only come from audience involvement. Our inspiration came from the Legislative Council.

Established in 1907, Legco was initially a completely white affair, with debates on such issues as eggs and plumes of ostriches: people were not allowed to take eggs from natural nests or capture natural ostriches, to protect licensed ostrich farmers. There were also, of course, more sinister debates to forge laws that consolidated Kenya as a white man's country.

Alliance had a long history of contact with this august institution. Even before the school was founded, its backers were closely associated with it. Dr. John W. Arthur, a missionary and a central player in the Alliance of Missions that had set up the school, was appointed representative of African interests. He guarded his status as the African voice jealously and was horrified that nationalists like Harry Thuku and Jomo Kenyatta would want to set up their own political organizations instead of joining the loyal associations that Dr. Arthur organized. He was a kindly person and obviously dedicated to his mission, but he acted as if he knew Africans better than they knew themselves. It was not until 1944 that the government appointed the first African representative of African interests, Eliud Mathu, Alliance class of 1928 and later a teacher there. Students, too, were involved in the colonial body: whenever a new session of the Legco opened, the school sent two boys as ushers. In 1955 it was Peter Mburu, of the debating society, and Bethuel A. Kiplagat, our Dorm Two prefect.

By 1957 Mburu and Kiplagat had left Alliance, so there was nobody in the committee with any personal experience of the legislative procedure. But we knew that it was modeled on the British Houses of Parliament, which we had studied in class, and we decided to change our debating format into our interpretation of the Parliamentary system. The dining hall became our parliament. The chair, a mallet of authority in his hand, became Speaker of the House. The audience would constitute ordinary members of Parliament, evenly divided between the government and the opposition. Once the principal proponents and opponents had spoken, it was the floor's turn. But they could not make a statement directly. They could only ask questions so as to expose holes in the position of the mover or that of the opposition, or help beef up any of the earlier responses. Skillful questions and follow-ups could really bring out contradictions in the positions of the speakers. If an ordinary member of the house disagreed profoundly with the position of either side, he would demonstrate this by crossing the floor. Whether they spoke or not, everybody was a participant. The constant to-and-fro across the aisle created drama, the crossings often greeted with clashing calls of shame or welcome, keeping the speaker constantly busy with his mallet.

Soon the Franciscan binary grouping of political actors into statesmen and scoundrels entered the lexicon of the debates. Initially the words provoked laughter because everybody knew that they were a good-humored dig at Carey Francis, but later they took on a life of their own, becoming descriptions of radical versus conservative positions. Scoundrels were more popular than statesmen, providing more drama with their extreme though often frivolous questioning, drawing applause, whistles, and boos from the audience. The speaker would call out order, order, lecturing the audience on parliamentary decorum and threatening to have the recalcitrant ejected by the sergeant at arms. One speaker always prefaced his answers with the Churchillian phrase *As I was saying before I was rudely interrupted.* And on another occasion: *Do you realize, sir, that your answer is a riddle, wrapped in a mystery, inside an enigma?* Thereafter speakers outdid one another in borrowing phrases from politicians in and outside the country.

Two debates stood out under the new format. *If you want peace, prepare for war* was the motion, which I was to move. Although I did not believe strongly in the proposition, rhetoric was more important than personal conviction. My main thesis was that if a people don't prepare for war, they become an easy target for the warlike, while those who prepare have a means of defending themselves. Then one could negotiate peace from a position of strength. Arming oneself acted as a deterrent, as in the Cold War between America and Russia. I concluded with the Machiavellian maxim *Hence it is that all armed prophets have prospered and all unarmed have perished,* a kind of *Dawa ya moto ni moto.* With more people crossing the floor to our side, we were clearly winning. The warrior seemed to inspire more awe and admiration than the peacemaker.

But a peacemaker intervened at a strategic moment. You harvest what you plant. You don't plant potatoes and expect to harvest corn. If you want war, prepare for war. If you want peace, prepare for peace. When my turn came to summarize, I could not put the slightest dent in that graphic image.

All in all, our interpretation of the parliamentary system worked for our needs, livening up the debates. Little did I know that a few years later the format would intervene in my life in the most unexpected of ways.

38

The August break, which began on July 31, brought good news to our family. My brother's wife, Charity Wanjiki, came home from Kamĩtĩ Maximum Security Prison, and we learned that Good Wallace had been relocated to the last post on the pipeline, literally next door to our village.

The pipeline was the system the colonial state had devised for releasing those held in the concentration camps. Those who refused to cooperate with their interrogators, despite attempts to break them with words or torture, remained held in the harshest camps; those who showed degrees of cooperation were moved in stages, until they were finally released to the camp nearest their home, before their reentry into the concentration villages. My brother was deemed cooperative after declaring that he had accepted Jesus as the ruler of his life. Good Wallace had never seen any contradiction between Christian values and those of liberation. As far back as I could remember, he had read the Bible avidly and regularly attended Sunday services at the African Orthodox Church before it was banned.

I had not seen him since that day he came down from the mountains by night, an armed guerrilla, to wish me success in my end of the primary school exams. I put on my Alliance uniform to show him that his prayers and wishes had been met. He was together with other prisoners but was allowed to come to the wall of barbed wire. Ngenia was not a heavily fortified prison: who would want to break prison on the last stage of their release? Still, the state wanted to make sure that the freedom fighters were seen as captives, common criminals, and not the heroes of people's political imagination. But Good Wallace would always be a hero to me. I fought back tears of joy, tinged with sorrow at the sight of him caged. He was quick to note my khaki shorts, shirt, and blue tie. The look and the smile on his face spoke of gratitude and satisfaction, as if the uniform were worthy of all the suffering he had undergone. As we parted, his older-brother instinct kicked in: he reminded me to take off the uniform and wear regular clothes so as not to get it soiled and ruffled. This assertion said it all. He had survived police chases, the mountains, and concentration camps. He was alive and well.

My reunion with Good Wallace was followed by another break without mishap. I met with the group of boys and girls I had been trying to organize. After much discussion, we decided against a debating club: we wanted an activity that might also attract our parents. We settled on songs for a possible December performance. During the term we could not all meet together, so we arranged ourselves into groups on the principle of proximity: those from the same school would practice together. With everybody having learned the songs, it would be easier to put everything together whenever opportunities arose for the entire group to meet.

When I returned to Alliance for my third term on September 5, 1957, I felt good that I had put in place a performance group to improve the social life of the new village. But the biggest satisfaction came from memories of my brief reunion with my brother, despite the barbed wire between us.

39

On October 4, a month into the third term, the Soviets, or the Russians as we called them, launched *Sputnik I* into space—the first man-made, earth-orbiting satellite in history. For some reason, this did not make a splash at our school. But on November 4 everything changed. News reached Kenya, as it did all over the world, that the same Russians had now launched *Sputnik II,* and it carried a dog named Laika. This event raised a hue and cry from white people from all corners of the colony: the Russians had sent a dog to die in space.

At an emergency school assembly, Carey Francis condemned this premeditated cruelty. Some students could not understand how the death of a dog in space could spur such anger and grief. For me, Laika rhymed with Malaika, and it sounded as if an angel had been sent to space, but then angels dwelled in a heaven beyond the clouds. An angel sent to die in heaven?

Then I learned that Laika was actually a stray dog from the streets of Moscow. The Gĩkũyũ word for stray dogs, *ngui cia njangiri,* or simply *njangiri,* was also the word for the homeless and the irresponsible. Boys threw stones at stray dogs. Despite the fact that dogs had once bitten me, I never could stand their screams: they eerily evoked the cries of humans in pain.

In our new village, stray dogs turned into hordes of marauders roaming the streets, often fighting among themselves for leftovers. The hungry dogs became bolder, sometimes growling and snatching food from little children and old people. The colonial state must have been given the order to reduce their population because there came a time when, instead of boys chasing dogs for fun, it was armed home guards hunting and gunning them down. Hunting dogs became an official colonial sport. Three or four policemen could chase the dogs across hills and valleys, competing with each other to see who could bag the most. By zigging and zagging with speed, the dogs often frustrated their marksmanship.

During the entire anti-stray-dog campaign, I never heard of voices raised in protest. And now this outburst for Laika! Looking back on all the dogs killed in our village, I could not help noting the irony that a stray dog from the streets of Moscow had done what no human had ever done before; that though forced, a *njangiri* had been the chosen vehicle for dramatizing the dawn of a new age. Once again the street had demonstrated its power.

40

Mourners of the anticolonial resistance used to sing, sorrowfully though secretly, that when patriot Kĩmathi died, the moon and the stars shed blood. The moon was a crucial symbol in the Shakespeare play of the year, *A Midsummer Night's Dream,* which revealed the true magic of theater to me. Its plays-within-a-play structure; its overall fairy atmosphere, where fantasy and reality became each other in an abandon of passions of mistaken identities; and the use of love potions to confuse and clarify matters of the heart had a familiar ring to them, recalling the magic of African oral stories, where metamorphosis was a common feature.

I never wrote, directed, or played a major role in any play at Alliance, but it was the school productions that finally shaped my work with the Limuru youth group. We would be putting on a performance in two interrelated parts, which would end in the form of a Christmas pageant. The first part, a kind of musical concert that included many of the spirituals I had learned at Alliance, from Joseph Kariuki, was organized around the theme of new life. It was really a preparation for the second part, a reenactment of the journey of the magi. As the three kings carrying myrrh and frankincense entered Kamandūra church from the outside and walked down the aisle toward the altar, the concert group joined in the singing:

O star of wonder, star of light,
Star with royal beauty bright,
Westward leading, still proceeding,
Guide us to thy perfect light.

The perfect light came from a manger near the altar. To the traditional journey of the magi, I had added comic relief: a parallel pageant of local shepherds looking for a lost pregnant sheep, who are delighted when they spot the same manger. They take it that their lost sheep has given birth and is feeding its young in the manger. They are baffled when they find a human figure being talked about as a lamb. But when they learn that the newborn is a child of God, they join the other pageant in songs, celebrating the new life. This theme held together the mixture of spirituals, carols, and some songs based on traditional Gĩkũyũ melodies.

Nothing like it had been seen in Kamandũra. It became the talk of the church and the village. Led by Edward Matumbi, the elders later approached me to turn the group into the nucleus of a regular church choir. The invitation was tempting, but organizing such a disparate group would have been hard work and taken a lot of time, and we were not able to continue.

For me, the performance helped intensify my sense of connection with Kamĩrĩthũ.* But for many others, the vision of a new life amid the anticolonial war may have hit home in a way that I had not consciously intended: the spirituals and the carols embodied hope for a new life, a theme the dwellers of the new village could embrace whatever their side in the unfolding political struggle.

---

* This was the beginning of my interest in community theater, with consequences that would change my life. See *I Will Marry When I Want*, a play, and *Detained: A Writer's Prison Diary*.

1958

A Tale of Two Missions

41

From the first term of my last year at Alliance, our eyes and ears were mesmerized by the political drama as it played out in the streets and legislative chambers of the country. The drama peaked sharply soon after the March elections, which added six more African elected members under yet another revised constitution, the Lennox-Boyd Plan, to make a total of fourteen, achieving parity with Europeans for the first time.

While welcoming the six directly elected members into their midst, AEMO rejected the portion of the Lennox-Boyd Plan that provided for twelve specially elected members, four for each racial group, albeit on a common nonracial roll. Proportionate to the racial populations represented, a single European was assumed to be equal to hundreds of Africans. AEMO had learned well the tactic of agreeing to the positive portions of an agreement and then rejecting the sections they deemed detrimental to African interests. On March 25, literally a day after the elections, AEMO released a statement strongly denouncing the Africans who had offered themselves for the special seats, describing them as stooges, quislings, and black Europeans.

On April 16, the day of our first break, the state charged

the seven authors of the quisling document with defamation and sedition. The case, in the middle of our second term, became a cause célèbre, the word *quisling* taking center stage. Not even Philip Ochieng, the most fascinated by words among us, knew the meaning, and we had to reach for dictionaries, some of which were not particularly helpful. The word was loaded with irony. It was coined by the British press in the 1940s from the name of the Norwegian fascist leader, Vidkun Quisling, who collaborated with Hitler in the invasion of his own country. Churchill would later use the word in his 1941 address to Americans, evoking the flames of anger that burned among the British people against the brutal Nazi would-be invader of his country. Fifteen years later leaders of the Kenya Africans were using the coinage against those deemed to be collaborating with the brutal British invaders. The trial resulted only in fines of seventy-five pounds for each of the seven accused, but by then, the flames of nationalism were burning in the entire country.

The state's worst fears would soon come to haunt them. The drama on the street and in the legal chambers moved to a completely different level when, on June 26, on the floor of Legco, Oginga Odinga declared that Kenyatta and the others imprisoned with him were still the political leaders of the Kenyan people. Even his colleagues in AEMO were surprised and hesitant, and it took the groundswell in the country to make them come around to Oginga Odinga's position. He had brought the power of the street into the chamber of political decorum, and the street had won.

The subsequent rallying cry in the streets became *Uhuru na Kenyatta*.

42

The year may have been one of great political drama, but for us in Form Four, the greatest test of our entire educational lives, like the sword of Damocles, hovered over all our activities and thoughts. Every year of my life in the school so far had had its own internal dynamics. In the first year, I had looked forward to familiarizing myself with the school and settling down. In the second year, the sense that I belonged was affirmed by the presence of new freshmen. The third year had a serenity of ownership. By the beginning of the fourth year, one had learned fully how to negotiate the three sites that made the Alliance ideal: the chapel for the soul; the playing fields for the body; and the classroom for the mind. This triumph, however, carried a contradiction: now every activity was a swan song; every day that passed was one step closer to an unknown conclusion. Balancing thoughts of an uncertain future with those of how far I had come, Johnson Oatman's hymn that we sang in the chapel seemed to speak to my situation:

When upon life's billows you are tempest tossed,
When you are discouraged, thinking all is lost,
Count your many blessings, name them one by one,
And it will surprise you what the Lord hath done.

43

The collapse of our three-person cabal of the Balokole had uprooted my spiritual life from its previous mooring in a group. Though Omange and I continued meeting without E.K., the collective spirit was not the same. I sought refuge where I had always found it: in the chapel and the Sunday school. The interfaith chapel, with its gothic pointed arch, was built between 1933 and 1934. The chapel was meant to be a symbol of God's presence in the school, the motive power behind its work and service, but it would also be a continuing reminder of the unity between Alliance and the colonial state.

Our chapel had no resident chaplain but instead relied on guest laymen, reverends, and bishops. I was endlessly fascinated by the different characters behind the pulpit. Some preachers appealed to the heart directly; others, the mind; and yet others, a mixture of the two. Generally the services were serious, somber, and reflective, but they were also performances, for though the order of service was set, each featured speaker brought his own ways and mannerisms into the pulpit.

Such was the case when Reverend Handley Hooper, formerly of Church Missionary Society (CMS) of Kahuhia, led the service one Sunday in December 1956. Behind the pulpit, he stood tall, calm, and collected, nothing dramatic about him. Then, taking a plate to illustrate something, it slipped from his clumsy fingers and fell to the floor, breaking into pieces. I was aghast. Slowly, deliberately, he bent down and picked up the pieces, one by one. A heart that was ready for Jesus, he said, had to break to pieces in humility and repentance. The Holy Ghost would put the pieces together to create something whole. The breakage, though real, was an act. Those who had heard him before talked of other acts they had seen, different but equally effective in drawing attention to the central theme of his sermons.

The entire community of students, teachers, and staff had to attend the chapel, the basic way in which they expressed their commitment to the school's practical and spiritual ideal of producing faithful Christian servants. Work in the classroom, participation on the playing field, and voluntary extracurricular activities in the community were part of the process. Voluntary work best expressed the spirit of commitment because it carried no reward other than service itself. For me, the Sunday school, throughout my four years, became such a service and reward.

I don't know how I came to volunteer for Sunday school at Kīnoo, five or six miles away, rather than in the immediate neighborhood. Getting to Kīnoo was a test of will and determination. One had to cross Ndurarua River, and then many valleys and ridges, including Itukaria forest, to get there and then back, so attending Sunday school at Kīnoo meant a whole day.

I took over leadership at the end of 1957 and looked forward to my first Sunday as the leader of a new team of four. I knew the ritual very well. The pupils gathered together for

the preliminaries before breaking into separate rooms for
the different teachers and then reassembling for the closing
prayer, nearly always the Lord's Prayer. The leader guided
the opening and closing ceremonies. For the last three years
I had seen others do it with apparent ease and authority. I
could have gone through the routine blindfolded. But when
I stood up and all those expectant eyes were fixed on me, I
felt the weight of the moment. I was glad and relieved when
I finally came to the closing prayer, which now I announced
with authority. I was supposed to say the first line, *Our
Father who art in Heaven,* but nerves took over. I forgot the
line. There was an awkward silence. In desperation I said
just about any words that came to my tongue: Heaven forgive; give us Heaven. But the pupils were generous. They
ignored my confusion and sang the entire Lord's Prayer
from beginning to end.

I was a little shaken. I had thought that stage fright
applied to actors only, but now I understood. I knew the
prayer by heart, having first memorized it way back in my
elementary days at Kamandũra, and yet when the moment
came, I froze. It was a humbling experience and a lesson.
The rest of the Sundays in 1958 went smoothly, with parents and children in the area getting to know me as *Mwalimu*
and occasionally inviting me and my team to their homes.

Most students did not participate in Sunday school. In
the afternoon they would go about their personal business,
hang around the compound and study, visit home for those
who lived in the nearby neighborhoods, or walk to the valley
for dates with Acrossians. These boys had the most glam-
orous stories to tell in the evenings, as if taunting us with

what we, the Sunday scholars, had missed. Certainly no tale about teaching scriptures could successfully compete with those about adventures with nymphs in the famous magic valley.

But I was not about to give up my Sunday school for social outings. The eager faces of the children reminded me of the magic of my own Sunday schools at Kamandūra. Later my commitment was reinforced by my personal and dramatic experience of evangelical Christianity. The commitment preceded and survived the breakup of the cabal. Not once did the preparation for the exams of my life ever tempt me to quit Sunday school at Kĩnoo.

44

Not surprisingly, sports were a requirement at Alliance, for they educated the body in the same way that the classroom did the mind and the chapel the soul. Chess, though not a requirement, could contribute to character. Together they created the man strong to serve. Although from the time of Grieves's leadership sports had been important, it was Carey Francis who turned the playing field into a secular equivalent of the chapel. He brought to Maseno and Alliance the passion he had already acquired in his youth in England, where he captained soccer, cricket, and tennis teams. At Trinity College, Cambridge, he had been a member of the First XI soccer team.*

---

* First XI is equivalent to varsity.

I never stood out in any team sports. My lack of coordination was almost comical. In soccer, the ball seemed to deliberately avoid me or else pass me by, mocking my leg in the air. My hockey stick nearly always missed the ball. I did, however, excel at indoor games, even if they were not at the center of the Alliance ideal. Although they were deemed merely recreational, I found them formative of character, mind, and soul.

I had joined the chess club begun by David Martin in 1950. Not having come from a feudal order, I found its medieval characters of kings, queens, knights, bishops, footmen or pawns in their descending order of value, the highest to the lowest, all in defense of the king, strange, even confusing at first. But once I mastered the rules, I took to it. Nicodemus Asinjo, one of the best in my time, could think several moves ahead. He had early on discovered the power of the pawn; sometimes he would even sacrifice his queen for pawn and position, which he would use to devastating effect. It became a life lesson for me: even in the lowest of persons, there is great potential, or as the Gĩkũyũ proverb put it, heavy rains start with a drop. Chess, though, had few regularly active followers compared with other sports. For some it was too slow; for others it involved too much thinking and mental calculation. It was a war game and called for mental endurance and the ability to vary tactics within a strategic vision, the very reasons I liked it.

Table tennis, as we called Ping-Pong, was the other game in which I could reasonably hold my own. Here the greatest champions of my time were Philip Ochieng and Stephen

Ngũgĩ (on right) with Nicodemus Asinjo

Swai. They were artists with the paddle. To the repertoire of shots—forehand, backhand, loops, lobs, chops, spins, and smashes—they added quickness of feet and could retrieve the ball from any corner, whatever its speed and power, and return it with the arrogant ease of a champion. Sometimes they could wear down an opponent by their defense tactics alone. I never quite figured them out, and I lost to them more consistently than I beat them. When the two of them clashed, even players at the other tables would stop to watch two great artists at the height of their powers.

Every boy was expected to participate in real sports like soccer, hockey, gymnastics, and volleyball and take them as seriously as the chapel and the classroom. The interhouse and interschool competitions ensured wide involvement. Of course our bodies were not equally equipped for every sport, but participation was what mattered. Even the cheering spectator was an integral part of each performance.

Carey Francis was one of the most intense spectators, and he could be seen kicking the air in solidarity with a player, or grinding his teeth and stamping the ground when an Alliance player made a silly mistake. He also emphasized fairness and sharing the ball, and he was not amused by displays of individualism in soccer and field hockey. In victory, he wanted us to display humility, and in defeat, learn lessons that would lead to future success.

Track and field at Alliance was the crown jewel of body education and my favorite as a spectator and participant. I loved the aesthetics of jumps, and since my elementary school days, I had been fascinated by long races. The narrative, rhythm, and drama of the hundred- or two-hundred-yard dash were concentrated in a short time, like a story that ended before one had even savored the beginning. But the long-distance races, from the mile to the marathon, were like a long story, narrated and acted by the runner with his body. The collective narrative, unfolding slowly and gradually rising in tempo, gave the spectator time to follow the tactics of the various runner-characters, heightening the spectators' expectations of what happened next.

I represented my house in the junior section in the high jump, unsuccessfully, but in the mile, I could just about hold my own. The mile and longer races were a wrestling match between the determined spirits of the will and the persuasive devil of surrender. I learned this in my very first cross-country race. The entire school took part. In the initial yards, we all ran as one mass. But as we went further down the slopes of Alliance, along the valley and up through other ridges and planes, the mass of competitors gradually separated into groups. I tried to keep up with the leading group. I felt good, proud. And then, suddenly, I started hearing inner whispers for me to slow down. The temptation was strong, almost paralyzing in its appeal. I would ignore them, only for them to return with greater and greater vigor as we approached the end. Finally I hearkened to the call, slowed down, and then walked, hoping that this would rest my feet and rekindle my energy. It did not. It was as if my legs were suddenly made of lead. Soon almost all the groups that had been behind me caught up and passed me.

In the next race, I fought against the demons, willing myself to take the next step, always seeking to catch up with the ones in front but never succumbing to the whispers of surrender. I finished in the top twenty and maintained this position. But the little demons never relented. Each race was simply a renewal of the struggle, the temptations increasing the more determined I became. It was this effort that made me understand why the metaphor of running the good race was so central to the Franciscan Christian ideal. Years later running would become an important symbol in my books, especially in *A Grain of Wheat*.

45

Alliance competed with many schools, which, in Kenya, were then separate and unequal. Educational performance across the three racialized categories was not easy to compare, and so sports acquired a symbolic value as the only way of comparing abilities. But race consciousness remained a factor in every aspect of any encounter between whites and blacks, particularly in the sports arena.

The one soccer event that lasted in my mind, though I was only a spectator, did not even involve the rival schools: it was a once-only match between the Alliance team and a well-known European club, the Caledonians. It was a home match, and I remember Carey Francis impressing upon us the importance of politeness, win or lose. There would be no dishonor in defeat by such a team; the chance to play against the Caledonians was its own honor and reward. He repeated the ban on a popular applause line: if you miss the ball, don't miss the leg.

Whether intended or not, the prep talk had the reverse psychological effect. The Alliance boys played as if they were possessed. Holding the Caledonians to a draw in the first half, the Alliance spirit rose tenfold, while the Caledonian fell by the same. In the second half, Alliance was the first to draw blood and kept up the pressure. In the last minute or so of the match, Hudson Imbusi stopped a shot at the Alliance goal with his foot. Everybody expected him to dribble a little, then kick it deep into the enemy side, but instead, hunted and attacked from all sides, Imbusi dribbled the ball across the entire field and scored, just before the whistle. The solo performance, an exclamation point, was greeted with thunderous applause from our school and gloom from our opponents, who left the field with bowed heads. A draw would have been a moral victory for Alliance, but an outright win? Carey Francis, the great believer in teamwork, thought the solo act foolish, very foolish, but even he did not seem too upset by it. The Alliance win was a big boost to our self-esteem: if we could beat a semiprofessional team, white schools like Duke of York and Prince of Wales would be nothing.

Yet the triangular sports between Alliance, Duke of York, and Prince of Wales became more like a duel between white and black than simply a routine athletic competition. Consciously so or not, every sports event between white and black became a metaphor for the racialized power struggle in the country.

Social and academic contact with Duke and Wales, outside sports, might have made a difference, but these were minimal, consisting of occasional attendance by a few students at each other's musical concerts and theater performances. Hosts and guests were polite, but there was no natural mingling. Some classes from Alliance and Wales would visit each other's school, hosted by their counterparts. They were like arranged debutante parties, with hopeful parents hovering around in expectation. The practice was abandoned. It may have been on such an artificial occasion that I first talked, one on one, with Andrew Brockett, from Prince of Wales, for my first social exchange with a white student. It was brief. I would have forgotten the incident, name and all, except that months later in my final year, we met again at a voluntary service camp.

46

Multiracial volunteer work and youth camps, being a new phenomenon, were not on the same scale of value as scouting, climbing Mount Kilimanjaro, or excelling in sports. Involvement in them carried no expectations of public accolades. And yet I was drawn to them. It could be that I was still looking for a community to replace the home I had lost or was simply responding to their novelty or the mood of the times.

The change-is-in-the-air mood was manifest in efforts by good-willed souls to bring the different races together to make up for the years of separate development. Bodies like the United Kenya Club and the Capricorn Society spearheaded these better-late-than-never goodwill missions. They saw change as a question of inviting Africans, qualified by education, property, and manners, to wine and dine with the like-minded and the like-placed of other races. Other experiments tried to bring white and black youth together through volunteer youth camps.

I don't know how Mutonguini came to be chosen as the location of this multiracial, multiethnic experiment. The area had a historical and geographic significance, being part of the region that connected the Kenya heartland to the coast, and had many students at Alliance. But the most dominant personality of the region was Kasina Ndoo, an ex-military man, a colonial chief so loyal to the British state that when once offered a reward of his choice, he begged for the Union Jack. He had also demonstrated inner courage in overcoming personal adversity: on returning from the coronation of Queen Elizabeth II in 1953, a neighbor had chopped off his hands. It was not known if the motive was jealousy, political protest, or vengeance, but the amputation did not deter him from active and loyal service to the colonial power.

The Mutonguini Camp was organized by some white Quakers from Western Province. Of the three Alliance volunteers, I was the only one from outside the area. Indeed, the expected diversity did not materialize. There was not a single Asian, and Andrew Brockett from Prince of Wales was the sole white student. He and I recalled our brief encounter at Alliance. He had already completed school and was waiting for admission to Oxford to study history. I was curious as to why he had joined the work camp in a completely black African area. He confessed that he chose volunteer service not for the pure love of it but to avoid taking a job in the colonial administration, enforcing unjust laws. I didn't mention it, but I couldn't help wondering if the youth, Johnny the Green, who once stamped my passbook papers and from whom I escaped, could have been such a student.

This led us to discuss racial issues, in terms not of economy and politics but of psychology. Social apartheid bred misunderstanding, which stoked the fear of the unknown, which in turn bred even more misunderstanding, in a vicious circle of endless mutual suspicion and animosity.

We agreed that greater social contacts could lessen racial tensions and stereotyping, our way of expressing satisfaction with the work camp. Years later, in my novel *Weep Not, Child,* the scene would reappear as the brief exchange between the fictional Njoroge and Stephen, relocated to a school compound.

The majority of the camp participants came from the Quaker-run Kamusinga High School in Western Province. I had met some of them before, as members of the Kamusinga choir that had once visited Alliance en route from a musical event in Nairobi. They were a truly joyous lot. They burst onto our compound as if hosts, not guests, announcing their arrival with singing:

We are happy and a-jolly
Like the monkeys on the trees
We are happy and a-jolly
Tonight.

They treated the body of their truck as a mobile drum, banging it in rhythm with their catchy tune. It was their energy and passion that made the melody live long in my mind. The group from Kamusinga at the Mutonguini Camp—among them David Wanjala Welime, David Okuku Zalo, Alfayo Ferdinand Sandagi, and Mabati Litaba—brought onto the site the same kind of energy and enthusiasm. The relationship between them and their white teachers seemed much more relaxed and interactive than any that I had seen before.

Our project involved constructing a social hall, the heart of what would become Mutonguini Community Center. From the European Quakers, already skilled in masonry and carpentry, we learned how to make bricks, bake them, make walls, and use theodolite and other tools of masonry and carpentry, a process that brought back memories of my days at Good Wallace's workshop in Limuru. After a hard day's work, we played soccer and volleyball with the community, often challenging local teams, not always successfully. Sometimes we had social evenings of discussion, again with the community. These quiet moments, the church services conducted by the local minister of the African Inland Mission, and our weekly excursions and climbing in the surrounding hills helped forge a genuine community spirit.

It was not my first time interacting with Akamba people. Although there had traditionally been border skirmishes between our two communities, the relationship between us was mainly one of trade. I remembered itinerant Akamba women traders being received by my mother and welcomed to stay for a night or two on their way to the next stop. This time I was part of their community. A few of the elders often came to our site. They were very much like the Gĩkũyũ elders I had known. I spoke Gĩkũyũ and the elders spoke Kikamba, two cognate languages. Precisely because of that similarity, however, there were some linguistic misunderstandings.

The elders, who seemed to genuinely like me, interspersed their address to me with the word *mutumia*, which in Gĩkũyũ meant woman. Why are they calling me woman?

I wondered, troubled. But neither in their tone nor in their body language could I detect any hint of malice or insult. Eventually I confided my unease to Stephen Muna, my classmate from Alliance, a resident of Mutonguini who, though he did not sleep at the camp, participated in the daily activities. He laughed at my predicament. *Mutumia* in Kikamba meant elder, not woman: they were showing me respect, accepting me, a young man, as one of them.

It was also during the camp that I learned and experienced the power of the drum. The drum was not a central musical instrument among the Gĩkũyũ as much as it was among the Akamba. One evening we heard the sound of a drum calling us to see the famed Akamba acrobatic dancers in their home area. We decided to go to the arena. It was pitch dark, the stars and moon the only sources of light. It did not matter. The insistent sound was clear and near. We followed the road toward Kitui town. Every time we rounded a corner or climbed up a ridge, thinking that was where the sound came from, we would be disappointed: the sound seemed to come from the next hill. Some gave up and went back to camp. Eventually only Welime, Okuku, and I were left, now determined more than ever to get to the source of this power.

After many miles of walking, we managed to trace the source to a bush off the road. Before us was a clearing, in the middle of which was a fire, and around the fireside some young men were drumming and others dancing. It was not the large spectacle we had imagined: these were neighborhood youth, out in the night. With my Gĩkũyũ and Welime's Kiswahili, we were able to explain ourselves. They welcomed us and continued drumming and dancing but now with greater vigor: they had a foreign audience in their midst. Our presence and obvious interest had injected a new life into what for them had been routine practice and self-entertainment. But still, for a time, there was nothing out of the ordinary. We were about to leave when the dancers we had thought cautious started doing somersaults in the air, sometimes two of them crossing in the air in skillful aerial acrobatics, made more mysterious by the firelight in the dark. Possessed, the drummers' upper bodies shook as if they held no bones. Then they too jumped in the air, in turns, holding the drums tightly between their legs, hands still beating rhythmically. It was as if they were in contest, propelled higher and higher by the competing powers of their drums. Then suddenly, peace. The fire was now just red embers. They were obviously enjoying the gasps of admiration from their visitors. When the time came for us to leave, they told us that we were actually on the outer edges of Kitui Town. A drum at night can sound deceptively near, I learned. Thereafter I would always associate the Ukambani region and the Akamba people with drums by night and aerial maneuvers against a background of encroaching darkness, held in check by the glow of red embers.

47

I had enjoyed the communal experience so much so that when later the same year I heard of another youth initiative, organized by a new body, Kenya Youth Hostels Association, I promptly signed up. The camp was a weekend affair, intended to be the first of a projected series that would bring European, Asian, and African youth together. Participants were asked to bring the barest of beddings: it would be an education in survival, not an indulgence in luxury. I borrowed a bike from my half-brother, Mwangi wa Gacoki, and reached the site, in West Limuru, on a Friday evening. It was the longest journey I had ever undertaken on a bike.

The site was on an escarpment, in an abandoned railway station built in 1899. A rail track was half buried under the earth, still visible through the grass that had grown around and over it. Altogether the place looked forlorn, not a single hint of its old glory. I had hoped to find and interact with boys from all over Kenya, a much bigger affair than the one in Mutonguini. Instead, I found only an Indian boy, Govinda, and two European instructors, one from the church and the other from the army. The army man, young, still in his military khaki pants and shirt, walked with the swagger of his trade. He made me recall the officers who had once beaten me in 1954, as well as the ones who had interrogated me in the 1956 Nairobi Saturday fiasco. In my mind, I named him the General. He had come in a Land Rover piled high with sleeping bags and other tools of survival. The churchman had come in his car. He was a bit elderly, in a safari jacket over a long-sleeved shirt. I named him the Archbishop. What a contrast: while the General walked as if he owned the earth, the Archbishop trod gingerly, as if afraid to hurt the ground under him. The General and the Archbishop had expected many more participants, at least more than this frail-looking Indian youth in long pants and his African counterpart in an Alliance uniform.

The Friday evening was a prep talk for Saturday, then into our different camp beds in the enormous hall, probably haunted by the spirits of hundreds of Indian workers who had lost their lives laying the railroad in this extremely steep escarpment that ended in the yawning Great Rift Valley below. Govinda and I talked about the adventures awaiting us on Saturday, even making a virtue of our numbers—we would get their undivided attention. But early the next morning Govinda collected his stuff, got on his bike, and left. Now I had two instructors all to myself. I would have their completely undivided attention, I consoled myself.

Armed with a map of the area, we trekked into the bush early Saturday morning, to learn to read maps and follow trails in the forest and other tips of survival. It was more like a scout camp without the name and with only one recruit. There was very little interaction between us. I just walked with my map in my hands, my two instructors reduced to talking to each other, except when I missed a trail, and the General would explain to me where I had misread the map or failed to notice small but significant landmarks. It was quite exhausting, moving up and down the slopes in the woods, with nothing but a couple biscuits and water to eat and drink.

Once, while a few steps ahead of them, I overheard a heated debate between them about Mau Mau guerrillas and government forces. It was then I realized that even they had not known each other before and that they held profoundly different views on what was going on in the country. They disagreed, for instance, on the colonial policy of collective punishment. The Archbishop argued for individual accountability, while the General asserted that there was no other way of dealing with natives so given to secrecy. They increasingly based their arguments on hypotheticals. If you knew that one of them held information that would save or endanger lives and that he was hiding among the group, it would be prudent to hold the bloody lot to account, the General asserted. What then was the difference between what the colonial forces were doing and what Hitler did during the Second World War? the Archbishop countered. On and on they continued. I was invisible.

Suddenly I realized that they had stopped walking and stood facing each other. The exchange had moved from mental confrontation to the threat of physical combat. The elderly, slightly mustached Archbishop would be no match for the younger, clean-shaven army General, yet he was rolling up his sleeves. The sight of them about to duel with fists in the forest was ridiculous. I stood there, completely mesmerized. How could I intervene between two white people at war? Then I had a vision: I thought I saw the man of God in a black cassock, a white collar around his neck, holding a huge Bible in front of him, as a shield against a gun pointed at him by a heavily armed military officer. It was so real that I felt terror. I coughed. They froze. The cassock, the Bible, and the gun were in my imagination, but my coughing had worked. They pretended that they were simply talking. I should go on till I came to another track, the General said. They followed me in silence.

When we returned to camp, I got on my bicycle and fled, a three-day hostel reduced to a single night and a day.

48

My mother used to tell me that traveling outside one's home made a person realize that it was not only his mother who cooked tasty food. The volunteer youth initiatives confirmed that, despite their disappointments. Alliance, too, showed me the truth of it in relation to Kenyan communities.

Right from the start, Alliance's national spirit was contrary to the state's policy of dividing Africans along ethnic lines, and the school accepted students from different communities. But under Carey Francis, recruitment into Alliance on a countrywide basis became a consistent policy in theory and practice. North, central, east, west, and southern coastal Kenya were all represented on the Alliance compound. Most important, the African staff came from different Kenyan communities and were revered or reviled purely for their individuality, not for their ethnic origins.

This was the situation that prevailed at Alliance throughout my four years. In Limuru, many workers of different
communities had come to our home, but they were visitors.
This was the first time that I was living, interacting, competing, and quarreling on a daily basis with such diverse
individuals. There was something to learn from every ethnic community and every person.

Of all the school captains of my four years, I found
Bethuel A. Kiplagat the most intriguing. His personality
seemed to transcend ethnicity. He was not readily identifi-
able with any one community. I once asked him about his
middle initial: he told me it stood for Abdul. He used to be
a Muslim before converting to Christianity. But why do you
retain the name Abdul? I asked him. Because it is also my
name, part of my life, he told me. Intriguing in a different
way was the lovable Samuel Mũngai, the 1958 captain. He
was very conflicted, not sure if he was a rebel or a leader. He
enjoyed his cigarettes and other pleasures and often broke
the rules that he was supposed to enforce. He was also a
ladies' man, who left a trail of broken hearts and a few in
the family way. Though he would not have scored highly
in the official moral estimate, he somehow held the school
together. Altogether I learned that just as good leadership
came from individuals of different communities, so also did
mischief, troublemaking, and bad leadership.

I became a dorm prefect in 1957, a leader of the diverse
communities in Dorm Two, Livingstone House, succeeding
G. Shokwe. Shokwe, a Mtaita, loved boxing. He used to take
part in amateur bouts in the lightweight division in Nairobi.

He also led the boxing club in the school, and he had often tried to make a boxer out of me. Eventually I agreed to go in the ring. I looked good, to myself at least, in the red gloves of a boxer. In my very first swing, I hit my more experienced, if thin and gangly, opponent on the cheek. The blow caught both of us by surprise. He fell down. I was horrified. I took off my gloves and left them, never to return to the ring. I just couldn't see myself as victorious for hurting another, even in sport.

My appointment as a dorm prefect was equally and totally unexpected. I had never consciously behaved in a manner that courted such a consideration, but I took it in stride. Conscious that I was in the same dorm where Moses Gathere used to wake us up with his lines from *Macbeth*, I toyed with the idea of using another quote from Shakespeare but varying the lines *to be or not to be,* to become *to wake or not to wake.* I never actually tried it.

Dunstan Ireri was the first to challenge my leadership. We had entered Alliance the same year and were friends, but Dunstan considered himself a rebel and expressed this by smoking, often stealing from his bed early in the morning or late at night to smoke down by the bush or the latrines. There was a smoking fraternity at Alliance, with members from all the dorms and ethnic communities. Some prefects had elevated smoking to the worst breach of school rules and would themselves mount invasions of the smokers' dens. The smokers and the prefects had a running battle of hide-and-seek, which the smokers talked about in terms of adventure, full of evasive maneuvers and narrow escapes.

I decided to deny Dunstan and the other smokers that pleasure. I did not see it as my duty to sneak up on people in their hideout. I drew a line in the sand. Smoking was forbidden within the dorm and the compound. What they did in the bush outside the school compound was their business. Though nobody of course admitted to being a smoker, I sensed that quite a few in my dorm appreciated the boundaries that I had set. But for one or two others, the end of the game of hide-and-seek spoiled the drama and the fun. Dunstan let it be known that he had been out smoking, and with every provocative behavior, he drew a crowd of admirers. And then he tried smoking under the cover of his bed. He did not really think I would punish him, but I made a stand. The entire dorm was behind me. Dunstan had to spend one whole Saturday cutting grass as punishment for smoking in the dorm. This became my style of leadership: making people stand with me in enforcing rules that affected the community. But even in this I tried to exercise judgment and not exert a sledgehammer on every breach of rules. I liked discussing rather than proclaiming rules and shouting threats. I needed the members to see that in a functioning community, everyone had to be accountable to one another. It did not always work, but it made my tenure as prefect tolerable.

49

My interest in different communities drove me into the activities of the Inter-Tribal Society, of which I became chairman, for some time. Leaders of various clubs used to make announcements to members during evening meals at the dining hall. I always had difficulty enunciating *Inter-Tribal Society*, swallowing the letter n, making it sound as if I were calling on members of the *Itertribal* Society or Eat-a-Tribe Society, to do this or that, which always provoked laughter. Members met regularly to exchange views on a whole range of issues, drawing from our different cultures to illuminate them. How was leadership organized in our different communities? What about the rites of passage? The society invited outside speakers and sometimes organized discussions with speakers drawn from its members.

I valued talks with individual students, outside the formal classroom or house affairs. Evanson Mwaniki, who had taken over from King'ori as the school pianist, told me a lot about church music. It was from him that I first heard of middle C on the keys of the piano. Mwaniki was shy, but when it came to playing the piano, he was very expressive. He did not have formal training in music; he just picked up his piano knowledge from his two predecessors, reinforcing my positive attitude toward learning from one's peers. I got more Kiswahili from David Mzigo than from Dollymore, the master who taught Swahili. Mzigo was a native speaker;

Dollymore had picked it up while stationed in Mombasa as a soldier during the Second World War. Discussions and arguments on history and literature that I held with friends, and the math exercises that I did outside the classroom, greatly added to my insights, sometimes proving useful in tests and exams.

The national awareness forged in school was also being replicated in the country, through the social struggles led by the nationalists in the mountains and now in the streets of Nairobi. One Nairobi Saturday, I took Joshua Omange and Nicodemus Asinjo to the new village that I was increasingly calling home. Once again my mother's roasted potatoes proved a winner. On the way back, I met an old lady reputed to be a stalwart nationalist. People said that her head was not well because she would sing banned resistance songs openly. Her back was bent; she walked with the support of a walking stick. After greetings, I told her my two friends, Omange and Asinjo, were both Luo. She touched her heart in blessing. These days there's no Luo or Gĩkũyũ, she said. We are all the children of Kenya.

We are all the children of Kenya. All the children of Africa. All the children of the world. Even though she has long passed on, I remember her words and looks and smile. It was another case of wisdom and enrichment from the street. Knowledge gained inside and outside a formal setting impacted my life equally.

50

The school library was one of the best and richest outside-the-classroom sources of knowledge. When Oades took us to the library in the first few days after my arrival at Alliance, I stood at the door, mesmerized by the sight of shelves upon shelves of books in a building devoted to nothing else but books: I had never seen so many in my life. I could not believe that now I could go in, borrow books, return them, and get some more as often as I wanted. I swore that I would read all the books in the library.

There was no guidance, but does one wait for a guiding hand when one is standing on the banks of a river, thirsty? One does not even worry about polluted sections: the water looks uniformly able to quench one's thirst. I read without any order, often led to an author by the quantity of their books on the shelves. I went through a number of G. A. Henty's historical empire-building heroics. Some of the titles, like *With Clive in India, or The Beginnings of an Empire* and *With Wolfe in Canada, or The Winning of a Continent,* put the imperial theme up front, the preface to *With Clive* promising *great battles to be fought, great efforts to be made, before the vast empire of India fell altogether into British hands.* Addressed to *my dear lads,* the intended youth readership, the preface could apply to most of Henty's tales of imperialism. I was interested in the fictional but not the historical details. The narratives became tiring, and they put me off such fiction for a long time to come. I abandoned Henty for a more consistently fictional world, or so I thought, in which characters were not bound by the realism of actual history. I wanted a world into which I could escape.

I thought I had found such a world in Captain W. E. Johns's series featuring James Bigglesworth, the pilot adventurer, whose actions I followed, wherever he went, whatever he did: *Biggles and Co.; Biggles Learns to Fly; Biggles Flies Again; Biggles in France; Biggles Flies East,* West, South, everywhere, it did not matter. Biggles was the hero of all seasons, places, and confrontations. It was only when I came to *Biggles in Africa* that I started feeling uncomfortable with the portrayal of non-English characters. Biggles was an RAF pilot, and he reminded me of the same force dropping bombs on Mau Mau guerrillas on Mount Kenya. His kind were trying to kill my brother. I did not have a developed view of what held me back; I just drifted away, this time into the fictional world of H. Rider Haggard.

The same odd feelings intensified. *King Solomon's Mines* was full of adventure but clearly at the expense of Africa. I had been brought up to respect old age as wisdom and experience, but Gagool was one of the most frightful depictions of an aged African woman I had ever encountered in fiction. She was evil, pure and simple, the genius behind the tyranny that had bedeviled Africa for centuries.

King Solomon's Mines reminded me of Stevenson's *Treasure Island,* for both had a treasure hunt at the center, but I was not able to wholly escape into Haggard's characters the way I had with Stevenson's. *King Solomon's Mines* could not stand without a savage Africa as the background; *Treasure Island* could stand without the savagery of the Pacific peoples. Looking back, I can see that Haggard and other popular writers, when it came to my continent, were penning from the same dictum: imperialism was normal, resistance to it immoral. Africa and its peoples were the background that enabled European self-realization, the same theme that ran through our history lessons. The fast pace, turns, twists, mystery, and denouement sucked me into those adventures, but soon even these elements could not blind me completely to the negative implications of certain images and groupings of characters. Even in fiction I was not going to escape the theme of empire building. But then I stumbled into the crime thriller and detective category, and I thought, just maybe, I might finally escape into the realm of pure, untainted fiction.

For a time it was Edgar Wallace, with his fast-paced crime thrillers and detective mysteries, and nobody else. Then I discovered that once I had finished the story and knew all the hidden facts, I could not read any of the books a second time. The titles, characters, and places had different names, but the story remained the same. He did, however, lead me to more serious detective thrillers, where the feverish excitement and curiosity about what happens next was not everything. Characters could be more complex and add to the depth and excitement of a story. Thus I came to think of Sherlock Holmes, his friend Dr. Watson, and their address in Baker Street, London, as real. I read and reread any stories with Sherlock Holmes in them. I started looking at people, teachers, fellow students, acquaintances, for clues about their past or where they had just been, the way Sherlock Holmes did. I once tried it on a startled Omange one Saturday:

I see you have just come back from the Indian shops.

How do you know?

Well, you are eating a papaya. Papayas don't grow in any of the fields around the school. We get them from the Indian shops.

Wrong. A friend gave me it.

Yes, but he must have gotten them from the Indian shops.

Maybe, but that does not mean that I was there or even that I have just come from there!

Clearly I was better at reading Sherlock Holmes than playing him. But I did not stop trying to imitate him, even using a mirror to look for clues, although a mirror was no substitute for a magnifying glass. Sherlock was so real that he even dwarfed his creator. Robin Hood was the only other such character: I never cared who his authors were, I just read anything with his name on it.

51

In time I started looking at what I read in and outside the class more critically: none reflected my black experience. Then one day I happened to pick up Alan Paton's novel, *Cry, the Beloved Country,* the subject of one of Carey Francis's talks. It may not have been a thriller or a detective novel, but the story of Pastor Stephen Kumalo going into the city to look for his sister Gertrude and his own prodigal son, Absalom, could just as easily have unfolded in Kenya. The theme reminded me of the plot line in Kenneth's unfinished book. I even wondered if Alan Paton was black: how else could he capture so well the tone and the imagery of African speech?

Cry, the Beloved Country whetted my appetite for books that reflected my social reality, but the library did not meet my needs. On further search, I found several copies of *Up from Slavery* by Booker T. Washington. It was my first auto-biography. The similarities between the situation in the nineteenth-century American South and Kenya were eerily captured in Washington's story. Racial barriers to black progress were familiar; in Kenya we encountered the color bar in every walk of life. The difference between colonial-ism and slavery seemed a matter of degree. That was why his statements that black people had gotten more out of slavery than the whites made me uncomfortable. Compar-ing his racial situation with the colonial in our country, I asked myself, how could one say that Africans had gotten more out of colonialism than the whites who profited by it?

Though I had not worked this out fully, I had mixed feelings about Washington. His thirst for education, and his determination to do whatever it took to reach his goal, mirrored mine. I liked his ideas about hard work and self-reliance, for this was what my mother had always taught me. But I felt uneasy about his asking black people not to agitate for social equality: self-reliance and self-effacement were contradictory ideals.

I looked in vain for writings that I could identify with

fully. The choice, it seemed, was between the imperial narratives that disfigured my body and soul, and the liberal ones that restored my body but still disfigured my soul. I was not sure if I really did want to read all the books in the school library.

I grew more discriminating in my choice. My own awakening and the books I analyzed in class were influencing what I expected to find in a story in terms of depth and complexity of character, theme, and plot. In that sense, the classroom was affecting the outside. Still, the classroom could not give me enough. I still needed the outside. If I could not get texts that appealed to my body and soul, I might at least stick to the ones that appealed to the soul, no matter what time and social space produced them. I could not go back to thrillers, detectives, and adventures with my old innocence.

There were some storybooks that transcended their time and authorship. Grimm, Aesop, and Andersen: I read their stories over and over again without their ever losing their appeal. They came closest to the oral tales around the evening fireside with which I had grown up. They had a common magic quality; they renewed themselves in the rereading and retelling.

My heightened discriminating sense led me to *Wuthering Heights* by Emily Brontë. It opened my eyes to a dramatically different way of telling a story. With its many voices, it felt much the way narratives of real life unfolded in my village, an episode by one narrator followed by others that added to it and enriched the same theme. The story of Heathcliff and

Catherine Earnshaw as told by Nellie Dean and Lockwood took some time to unravel, but it was gripping and immeasurably sad. The winds of the Yorkshire moors reminded me of the frosty winds in Limuru in July. I never knew an author who could make the weather feel so real.

From Brontë, I drifted to Tolstoy. As in the case of Brontë, I knew very little about Tolstoy. But I had not gone far in his *Childhood, Youth,* and *Boyhood,* the trio in one volume, when I felt a desire I had never experienced, at least not with this intensity: I wanted to write about my childhood. Before, such feelings had been vague and fleeting, not calling for immediate action. This new desire was insistent. It would not even let me finish Tolstoy's book. I forgot all about my former arguments with Kenneth about the license to write.

It was 1957, my third year at Alliance. The story that came out of me was based on a belief we held as children that we could summon a loved one from wherever they were, by whispering their name into an empty clay pot. In the story, the fictional but autobiographical narrator's first whisper works: his auntie who lives thirty miles away turns up on the third day after the summons. Emboldened, the narrator is eager to display his new powers to an audience. The opportunity comes when he hears his mother complain that his older brother who works in Nairobi does not come home. He assures her that if she so desires, he can make him come home, no later than the third day. Of course his solemn declaration is greeted with skeptical laughter by the rest of the family, but he does not mind. His revenge would come: *When everyone was absent, I went to the kitchen. There was the cooking pot, mundane, disinterested, dead—but wait—possessing, as I knew, magical powers. Lifting it reverently from its hook, I slowly and deliberately called my brother by name.* But the magic does not work. That was the ironic twist. Following Tolstoy, I titled the story "My Childhood." It was a couple of handwritten pages, whereas Tolstoy's was a book, but I submitted it to the editors of *Alliance High Magazine.*

I did not get a response, not surprising as there was normally no editorial exchange between the writer and the editor, and I soon lost hope and forgot all about it. But when the magazine came out later, in September 1957, a friend spotted my piece. I could hardly wait to see and read it. It was my first-ever published work. In appearance, the nice print was a far cry from my handwritten version. It was of course smaller than the handwritten, but that did not matter.

Once I started reading it, however, I was appalled by the editorial license taken, and my excitement fell. The title had changed from "My Childhood" to become "I Try Witchcraft." That, I did not mind: the new title was pithy, though misleading because what I described was not witchcraft. But the second paragraph, an editorial insertion, had the fictional narrator assert that Christianity was without doubt *the greatest civilizing influence and as it crept in amongst the people, many began to see the futility of putting their faith in superstition and witchcraft.* A simple story, in which I had poked fun at our childhood beliefs and superstitions, had been turned into a condemnation of the pre-Christian life and beliefs of a whole community and, simultaneously, an ingratiating acknowledgment of the beneficial effects of enlightenment. I was turned into a prosecution witness for the imperial literary tradition from which I had been trying to escape. Although well intentioned, this editorial intrusion smothered the creative fire within me; no amount of reading of Tolstoy's *Childhood* and *Youth* would rekindle it. I did not feel pride in my creation.

52

During the holidays, I showed the piece to Kenneth. His sarcastic reaction was perhaps predictable: Did you first get a license to write?* He never would forget about our arguments. I could have responded that mine was not a book or that I was inoculated from censure by the editorial input of my teacher. But really, I no longer held the position that one needed a prior license to write. Even in our arguments during the Asante rally in Nyeri, I had begun to shift my position, and Tolstoy had inspired me out of it altogether. I conceded defeat. Kenneth did not offer his opinion on the quality of the piece. He was happy that it had won him an argument started in our elementary school, three years before. Now the victor of that argument, he would bring it up even in the presence of a third person, citing my story and indirectly inciting curiosity about it.

The piece garnered me two new friends who I would later

---

* The debate on the license to write is narrated in *Dreams in a Time of War*.

label my ological buddies, and the days of our intense association, my ological period. The first was Kĩmani Mũnyaka,
a junior high school graduate and now a primary school
teacher. His habit of always carrying a magazine or a book
with him had earned him the reputation of being a reader
of books. The moment Kenneth introduced us and brought
up the subject of my publication, Kĩmani wanted to read it.

I awaited his comments eagerly, hoping that he would
not dwell too much on the bit about the civilizing effects
of Christianity. I needed to hear an opinion on my actual
creation. His first words, when next we met, sounded at
odds with the subject: Do you know how to spell the word
psychology? I was puzzled: What did a spelling test have to
do with my story? The word was not even in my piece. To
put him in good humor, I tried to say the letters loudly. I
kept on getting the spelling wrong, and finally I gave up.
His lips, pursed in a smile, told me that he had been antici-
pating my failure. You see, the word begins with the letter
p, he explained with the patience of a superior, but don't
blame yourself too much, you did what most people do.
They forget that the *p* is silent, so all they hear is the sound
of the letter *s*. Now, about your story. The piece was quite
interesting. He paused. It manifests one of the pillars of the
psychology of desire. I did not know what he was talking
about. What had psychology, let alone one of desire, to do
with my story? I asked him.

Everything, he argued back. Psychology was in every
human action and behavior. It dealt with the hidden motives
behind them. You might think that your assembly of words

was just a story about whispers in a clay pot, but actually it was whispers into self, like the silent talks we all have inside ourselves. First you wrote it at Alliance, a high school, away from home. Correct? Yes. You were lonely, you were longing for home, mother's food, cooked in a clay pot. Your teachers were white, correct? Yes, but not all of them. True, but the principal was, correct? Yes. Remember that you were also surrounded by Christianity, a foreign religion. So you were clearly longing for something to make you feel at home. But the story was more than all these, he explained. It was really a story of the human desire to return to the womb, this clearly suggested by the persona in the story putting his head inside the pot. You know the Gĩkũyũ word for pot, *nyũngũ,* is exactly the same for the womb, correct?

This bit made me look at him strangely. First, I had indeed been looking for something to make me overcome the sense of loss and connect with the new village. Second, I had sometimes wondered what it had felt like to be in my mother's womb. I would try to recall my own life there, but I had not the slightest memory beyond what my mother told me about my having kicked her, quite often. Apparently, of all her children, I had been the most troublesome in the womb. Kĩmani seemed to be on to something. I listened, my curiosity aroused.

The clay pot, its mouth, narrow neck, and round chamber, obviously suggested the womb, he continued, unaware of my reaction. A person was most secure in the womb. Protected, nurtured, he has the most power. Would one long for security if one were already secure? he asked, piercing me with his eyes. The story is really about your loneliness and insecurity at Alliance. You probably have difficulty making friends. If you had friends to play with, you wouldn't have had the time or the desire to retreat into a make-believe world, correct? And you certainly worried too much about whether you, a boy from the village, could survive at Alliance. Before I could explain, he had assured me that he would help me. He would help me break worry before worry broke me.

He brought two books to our next meeting: Dale Carnegie's *How to Make Friends and Influence People* and *How to Stop Worrying and Start Living*. But he wouldn't let me borrow them to read on my own. He liked talking about them, retelling stories of success cited in them. The stories were always about people who started in lowly positions but rose to success, nearly always measured by wealth. One had started with a dollar but somehow, through single-mindedly pursuing an idea, he had risen to the top. There were hints on how to listen to people, how to let them talk about themselves while you listened. I found him and his stories extremely fascinating. I was a captive audience. He liked my company more than Kenneth's because Kenneth was more liable to argue back, even question his beloved Carnegie.

Soon I understood the source of Kenneth's skepticism. In time I noted that Kĩmani only talked about those two books. The reputation he had for reading was based on the fact that he always carried one or the other. He was not expansive about other topics, except as they manifested some aspects of psychology. Talk about education, he brought up psychology of knowledge. Talk about love or politics, he brought up psychology of power, love itself being a play of attraction and repulsion in the game of power. Had I not seen how even a big man becomes weak before a woman once his heart has been overpowered? He had some old copies of a biannual psychology magazine. It was like his personal talisman or proof that what he said was rooted in knowledge. We both lived in different parts of Kamīrīthū, but our paths crossed time and again. Whenever we met, he had a different psychological insight and then would quickly move on to stories culled from Carnegie.

Kīmani had a habit of reading a text, restating it in his own words, and then interpreting it by quoting instances from the same passage. His advice was always through quotes or paraphrases from this guru of wisdom, achievement, and success. And for a psychologist who advised on the importance of listening, he seemed to prefer talking to hearing. I started avoiding him. I really did not want to hear my story used as a bridge to Carnegie.

53

In contrast, I often actively sought the company of Gabriel Gaitho Kuruma, who lived in the next village, Kīhingo. Gaitho and I had worked together in the Christmas pageant that I had helped to organize the previous year. He taught the group the hymn "We Three Kings." He reacted to my story differently than Kīmani: he was sure that I was already a writer. He had completed two years of high school and was a graduate of Kagumo Teacher Training College. I don't know how we first met, but we had always been in conversation throughout my high school years.

Gaitho was a reader of books, with an interest in Pan-Africa and the world, and he and I had weeks of conversation, touching on different subjects. But he had a way of smuggling the name of Kwame Nkrumah into any theme or topic of our talks. He had followed Nkrumah's career from Lincoln University back to the Fifth Pan-African Congress in 1945, culminating in his role as a former prisoner who won Ghana's independence. Gaitho admired the philosophy of Marcus Garvey because Nkrumah had said that it had inspired him. He liked George Padmore and W. E. B. DuBois because they had allied with Nkrumah and Kenyatta in the 1945 Pan-African Congress in Manchester. It was from Gaitho that I first heard the quote *the problem of the twentieth century was the problem of the color line,* which he attributed to DuBois. And when the subject of Booker T. Washington and his book *Up from Slavery* arose, he pointed out that DuBois, Nkrumah's friend, had opposed Washington and founded the Niagara Movement, which later became the NAACP. He did not think much of Washington, although he could not quite put his finger on what irritated him. In contrast, he would tell over and over again the story of Rosa Parks, who had refused to give up her seat on a bus to a white man and so sparked the Montgomery bus boycott, hinting at some kind of connection between that and the Mau Mau–inspired bus boycott in Kenya.

In Kenya, Gaitho liked Tom Mboya because his Nairobi

People's Convention Party echoed Nkrumah's Convention People's Party. He talked about Mboya's rise from a trade unionist, to studying at Oxford, to being the brilliant architect of the tactics used by the AEMO. He knew in great detail every exchange between Mboya and Michael Blundell in Legco debates. But Mboya's greatest brilliance was his alliance with Kwame Nkrumah. Mboya had learned from the master. All brilliant African roads led to Ghana. It was from Ghana at the All-African Peoples' Conference on December 22, 1958, that the call for the release of Jomo Kenyatta became continental and global. Our own Mboya was chairman of the conference, a great honor for the Kenyan struggle. It was as chairman that Mboya called for the end of imperialism in Africa. Gaitho could quote, almost word for word, Mboya's call: *Whereas 72 years ago the scramble for Africa started, from Accra we announce that these same powers must be told in a clear, firm, and definite voice: Scram from Africa.* From scramble to scram: the speech made the twenty-eight-year-old Tom Mboya a household name in Africa. In the Kenyan press, this was reduced to a one-liner, *Mboya calls for whites to scram from Africa,* which Gaitho would add with satisfaction.

Despite his excitement over the independence of Ghana in 1956, Gaitho also argued that Ghana was not the first independent country in Africa, citing the cases of Ethiopia, Liberia, Libya, Tunisia, and Morocco, even hinting of an earlier independence of African peoples in a place called Haiti, though he did not elaborate further, and I did not know enough to counter his assertions and evaluations. Gaitho may have been the secondary school equivalent of

Ngandi of my elementary school days, but unlike Ngandi, he did not mix fact with fiction. While Ngandi told stories largely and would rely on story and rumor as his authority in support of the truth of the story he was telling, Gaitho talked mainly history and ideas and was more likely to cite the authority of a book or a magazine.

He admired philosopher-kings in politics. I could not tell who he liked more, Nkrumah the politician or Nkrumah the intellectual. Though impressed by Nkrumah's Pan-Africanism and commitment to a continental African Union government, evidenced by his vow to surrender Ghana's sovereignty to such a union, Gaitho talked with equal if not more enthusiasm about his idol's studies in philosophy and theology, among other pursuits. He had read Nkrumah's autobiography, *Ghana*, and knew that Nkrumah had given up the lure of worldly possessions that his education could have secured him, for a life of service. It may have been this aspect of Nkrumah's learning and dedication to service that led him to another intellectual who had studied philosophy and theology, among other things, and given up his academic posts in Germany for a life among the sick and the poor in Africa: Albert Schweitzer.

Gaitho talked about Schweitzer with genuine awe: a musician, a philosopher, a theologian, an expert on organs, and a medical doctor. Can you imagine him giving up all that to build a hospital in Lambaréné in French Equatorial Africa?* But it was not his philanthropy that most intrigued

---

* In the republic of Gabon today.

Gaitho: it was Schweitzer's thoughts on Jesus, the historical and the eschatological. I had never heard of the word
eschatological. He lent me Schweitzer's book, *Out of My
Life and Thought*. This was my second encounter with an
autobiography.

The quest of the historical as opposed to the eschatological Jesus dominated our discussions. Schweitzer's review of
the history of research on the life of Jesus, what he called
The Quest of the Historical Jesus, intrigued me. I would
have liked to have read a complete biography of Jesus, but
not coming across one, I was left with the bits and pieces
found in the four gospels of Matthew, Mark, Luke, and
John. The engagement with Schweitzer coincided with
my growing doubts about evangelical Christianity and its
stress on a personal experience of sin and a personal link
to Jesus. What Jesus? The Son of Man or the Son of God?
Jesus of the Sermon on the Mount or Jesus of the end of the
world and final judgment? From my experience, evangelical
Christianity placed too much stress on the end of the world,
the second coming, and judgment of sinners. Jesus the child
prodigy, who lived on earth, escaped with his mother into
Egypt, learned carpentry, walked with fishermen, cautioned
people not to judge else they would be judged, challenged
people to cast the first stone, and talked about service to the
least among us, was much more real and appealing than the
apocalyptic Jesus. I did not want to see the end of the world.
Or entertain the idea of people burning in hellfire from the
Day of Judgment to eternity.

And then Gaitho came up with a solution. The historical and the eschatological were one. The historical was the social experience of today; the eschatological, a vision of tomorrow. The historical Jesus foresaw the fall of Rome, the old world, and the coming into being of a new world. One order would give way to another. Imperial Rome and the social groups that allied with its domination would be judged. The historical Jesus was also universal because his message of the end of the old order spoke to all situations of the oppressor and oppressed, past, present, and future. We applied this to the colonial situation, where London was Rome and Governor Evelyn Baring, the modern Pontius Pilate. The home guards who worked with the colonial regime were the modern-day Pharisees. This was an eye-opener. The eschatological Jesus spoke to me: the colonial world was bound to fall. We shall be free.

This was of course our conclusion, not Schweitzer's. I often wondered about my enthusiasm for him. It was partly due to Gaitho's infectious passion. But I may have detected some parallels between him and Carey Francis. Both accepted Jesus as the center of their lives. Both had given up high academic positions for service in Africa. But Carey Francis was clearer that he wanted to serve *the least among us.* Schweitzer wrote autobiographies; Carey Francis would never do an autobiography or any writings that drew attention to himself. Schweitzer studied the life of Jesus; Carey Francis followed the life of Jesus. But on one thing they were completely united: service to the community driven by their relationship to Jesus, no matter what their interpretation of that relationship. My love of volunteer work may have been inspired by the devotion to service manifested in the lives of two disparate missionaries on opposite sides of the continent.

54

There was no way one could hide from Shakespeare at Alliance. His characters had become my daily companions, as were his insights into social conflicts. Inside and outside the classroom, over the last four years, Shakespeare was an integral part of my intellectual formation. I had come to understand Gathere's recitation of Shakespeare's *Macbeth* every morning.

I always looked forward to seeing which Shakespeare would show up at the end of the year. But the *King Lear* production in 1958 held more than the usual fascination: it was going to mark the end of one era and the beginning of another. I did not take part in the production, but I could not help but admire my classmate Andrew Kaingu's courage in auditioning for and accepting so big a role: Lear dominates the play in the number of scenes in which he appears and the lines he speaks. Kaingu had to cram all of this and appear in nearly all the rehearsals, while also preparing for Cambridge exams that would determine his future. But he did it. The last performance was an incredible feat of stamina and a convincing display of the whole gamut of emotions, from the comic to the tragic, in the life and actions of Lear.

Kaingu's hair had been powdered gray to give his nine-teen years a touch of age, but he did not need gray hairs to display his skills and talent. In the storm scene, with only the Fool and blind Gloucester as his audience, Kaingu's Lear rose to the occasion, mixing reason with palpable madness: *Plate sin with gold, and the strong lance of justice hurtless breaks; arm it in rags, a pygmy's straw does pierce it.* The lines and delivery captured the ongoing practice of colonial justice outside the walls of Alliance.

Shakespeare may have been beloved by the colonial establishment, pure art to be liberally dished out to schools, but his portrayal of blatant power struggles, like conflicts between the feudal and the new social order dramatized in *King Lear,* spoke directly to the struggles for power in Kenya at the time. The play accurately reflected the bloody struggle between the Mau Mau guerrillas and the forces of the colonial state. Fundamentally, Shakespeare, by exten-sion, questioned the assumed stability of the state; he dra-matized, for all the world to see, that power came from and was maintained by the sword. Shakespeare gave birth to student writers of drama: Henry Kuria, Kimani Nyoike, Gerishon Ngũgĩ, and Bethuel Kurutu.

But though they lacked obvious political themes, the stu-dents' efforts laid a foundation for a tradition of plays in African languages, Kiswahili in particular, and of theater as community involvement. While the English-language pro-ductions targeted school audiences and were often attended by the English-speaking colonial elite, the Kiswahili pro-ductions targeted the community as its main audience.

Still, it was Shakespeare who had inspired the local tradition, one that demonstrated, in practice, that Kiswahili was an equally legitimate vehicle of creative imagination.

55

Despite the welcome Shakespearean distraction, I had not forgotten the big academic hurdle still before me. Alliance had annually sent its graduates on to Makerere University College, in Kampala, Uganda, in numbers and regularity that attracted the admiring notice of even the most rabid intellectual settler-philes. A few Alliance graduates had secured places abroad, but the most coveted was admission to Makerere, which depended entirely on one's performance in fiercely competitive exams. I wanted to be among the chosen.

So for the rest of the year, I hid inside book covers and class notes. There were students who memorized dates when it came to history, formulae when it came to physics with chemistry, and facts of plant and animal life when it came to biology. And as before all other exams, some talked as if they were quite certain of the passages from Shakespeare, Bernard Shaw, or H. G. Wells, on which literature questions would be based. I was bad at cramming facts, worse at retaining and recalling them. I was more interested in understanding processes. So whenever I would hear other boys talk about geography or history, spouting these numerous facts and figures, I would feel slightly nervous, despite the fact that I had been through similar fears before.

In one area, however, I accepted and embraced challenge openly. All eight subjects, including math, were compulsory; one had to take an exam in each. But there was also one optional paper, additional math. It did not count for the final grade or college acceptance. It was for one's intellectual ego. Additional math was a notch higher and more challenging than the regular. Most students avoided it largely because of the reputed difficulty and quite frankly because it meant extra hours of preparation that could otherwise usefully go to what counted. On an impulse, I mentioned to my friend Joseph Gatuiria that I was undecided about taking additional math. Gatuiria laughed outright. There is no way you can pass additional math. You are not Asinjo, he said, referring to the best mathematics student in the class of 1958. Asinjo had more precision: my path to a solution meandered and was cluttered with debris, while Asinjo's was tidy and short. Gatuiria's skepticism became a challenge. I would take additional math.

The Overseas Cambridge School Certificate exams began Monday, November 24. But the final assembly and speech, starring Carey Francis, took place on Thursday, December 4, a day before the last paper. The scene was a little reminiscent of Jesus sending out his disciples to go and teach all nations, baptizing them in the name of the Father, and of the Son, and of the Holy Ghost. Carey Francis read our commission, the same, no doubt, that he had read to all those who Alliance had sent out since he took over the headship in 1940:

Go forth into the world in peace;
Be of good courage;
Hold fast that which is good;
Strengthen the fainthearted;
Support the weak;
Help the afflicted;
Honor all men;
Love and serve the Lord.

That was it. Formal divorce from the House of the Interpreter. So on December 5 I sat the last paper as an occupant of a liminal space, neither an Alliance nor quite an ex-Alliance; neither of the school nor of the world. After it I knew, without a shadow of doubt, that my Alliance days had ended.

One last piece of business remained to mark my final and formal severance from Alliance: the Leaving School Certificate. Carey Francis personally gave these out to each student, one on one. As I went into the office, I recalled all my previous encounters with him, on the grounds, in the chapel, the classroom, everywhere, for he was everywhere even when he seemed to be nowhere.

56

The fact is that the Alliance of my time was Carey Francis, and Carey Francis was Alliance. His personality was stamped on everything: the grass that was always well trimmed; the parades of cleanliness as second only to godliness; the tidiness of mind and heart reflected in the body

beaten into shape by sports and rigorous tests in endurance; the everyday of prayers in the morning to the preps
in the evening. It was stamped on the behavior of faculty
and students alike, especially in his presence. Even digni-
taries who came to the school, from the governor and high
government officials to visiting British MPs, put on an air
of gravitas in his presence. It was not that he demanded
obeisance; it was simply the way he lived his life as the head
of an Alliance Family and the reputation it had generated.
He ran the Family with the guidance of the only one master
he accepted and to whom he had pledged his obedience:
Jesus. In a 1944 letter to Reverend H. M. Grace about
S. G. Young, Carey Francis expressed what he expected
from teachers at Alliance:

> We need a man (indeed we need several) who has a degree,
> can teach, is ready to work, is game to turn his hand to any-
> thing that is needed. He must be more than a classroom
> teacher, must care for the boys. He must be a Christian—we
> try to make that (with very limited success) the centre of
> everything. I do not mind what brand so long as it is real,
> and so long as he is ready to work happily with those of
> other brands who serve the same master.

He was describing himself. His single-minded devotion to
that ideal gave him an inner stability whose weight could be
felt by those around him. He seemed every inch the Kip-
lingesque character who would walk with kings and yet not
lose the common touch, the rock that could not be moved,
by disaster or triumph.

Only once did I see a crack in the rock. It was the afternoon of Tuesday, February 22, 1958, during a visit by his old college mate at Cambridge, Bishop Stephen Neill. Even the way Carey Francis introduced him to us in Form Four A told us that he looked up to him. Bishop Neill talked about the Anglican Church, probably a summary of ideas in his book on Anglicanism. Suddenly, touched by some words Neill had uttered, Carey Francis began to weep, tears flowing down his cheeks. I could not tell what exactly Neill had said to move him so. Maybe it was the phrase *via media,* which would translate as the middle way between extremes, the core of the Franciscan outlook. Whatever the case, it was almost as if Neill had just come from a conference with Jesus and were delivering a message from Heaven. Neill did not seem surprised. He did not even change his tone of voice. He must have seen it before. But I was shocked. This was a face of Carey Francis I had never seen.

He embodied other contradictions. Once, during a math lesson, he said that in all his time at Alliance, he had met only one boy, David Wasawo,* who could be accepted in Cambridge on the basis of merit alone. And yet here was a person who devoted his life to making Alliance boys excel in whatever they undertook and was delighted when they beat the daylights out of Wales and York in anything competitive. In a talk that he gave at a joint meeting of the Royal African and the Royal Empire societies in London on March 31,

---

* Wasawo later graduated from Cambridge with a degree in mathematics and went on to teach at the University of Nairobi.

1955, he said that, apart from Africans coming from poorer, less endowed homes,

> they are essentially the same as English boys. They would bear comparison with those of the European schools in Kenya, or with a good school in this country, in intelligence, in athletic prowess, in industry, courtesy, courage, and trust-worthiness, and as gentlemen.*

He believed, as I would learn years later, that Mau Mau was "evil through and through, and has done much harm to African and European alike; but it is a resistance movement," waging a legitimate nationalist struggle against foreign occupation and "like resistance movements in the war [World War II], Mau Mau fights not only against European invaders but even more fiercely against African collaborators." He had faith "in the British Empire and the great traditions for which it stands." Indeed, he believed that the colonial administration, as opposed to the political white settlers, had integrity and was essentially well intentioned; yet precisely because of his faith in the empire, he led efforts in documenting proofs of wrongs done by the colonial forces and presenting them to authorities higher up the chain of command. In some areas, he had told the joint session of the Royal Africa and the Royal Empire societies, "the average Kikuyu has hardly known which to fear more, the Mau-Mau or the forces of law and order. By both,

---

* Edward Carey Francis, "Kenya's Problems as Seen by a Schoolmaster in Kikuyu Country," *African Affairs* 54, no. 216 (July 1955).

men have been robbed, beaten, carried off, and killed, and there is almost no hope of redress. They hardly try for it. To whom should they go?" He emphatically told them, "we shall never destroy Mau Mau by killing gangsters or imprisoning oath takers, we shall destroy it only by disposing of the foundations on which it rests by showing that we are not enemy invaders." He was truly a mystery.*

Now I was back in his office, facing, for the last time, the man whose shadow had fallen on the entire school during my four years. He asked me whether I knew what I was going to do, pending the Cambridge results. I would be teaching at a primary school called Kahũgũinĩ. Though I had never been there, I tried to explain where it was, but he beat me to it. Is that in Gatũndũ? I said yes. Then he gave me a prep talk about temptations out there in the world. He had one piece of advice: Whatever you do, don't be a politician. All politicians, black, white, and brown, are unmitigated scoundrels.

I took the piece of paper, a certificate based on how the school viewed each of the students. It vouched for character. Among the remarks, one jumped out: he has shown a pioneering spirit. I looked at Carey Francis. I did not see myself as a pioneer. But I valued this comment more than anything else, for it could only refer to my participation in work and youth camps. My activities at Mutonguini and the escarpment had been noticed. Thank you, Mr. Francis. Thank you, Alliance.

* Carey Francis, "Kenya's Problems," 190, 191, 194, 193, 192.

Outside the office, on the parade ground where I first disembarked on January 20, 1955, it hit me all at once. Now it was December 1958. The piece of paper in my hands simply certified that after four years I had forever left what Carey Francis used to describe as an oasis in a desert. The desert and the oasis produced each other. I had once seen it as a sanctuary surrounded by bloodhounds, but in time, over the four years, the howl of the hounds had quieted to a faint whimper. Now, outside these walls, were human voices that drowned or matched those of the hounds. I felt a mixture of delight and dread. I was leaving the walls to plunge into the unknown.

Alas, I had half forgotten that, outside the gates, the hounds were still crouched, panting, waiting, biding their time to pounce . . .

1959

*A Tale of the Hounds
at the Gate*

57

The saga of the hounds begins in April 1959, four months after I left Alliance. I am sitting by the window, a few seats from the back of a bus traveling from Nairobi to Limuru. At a roadblock near Banana Hills, the police wave us to a stop. Two officers, one wielding a machine gun and the other a rifle, rush in, shouting *don't move*. They imprint themselves in my mind as Messrs. Machine Gun and Rifleman. Mr. Machine Gun stands by the entrance to block anyone from exiting. Mr. Rifleman quickly walks up and down the aisle; then he relaxes, slings his rifle on his right shoulder, and starts demanding identity and tax papers, beginning with those near the entrance. Although there is nothing unusual about this in a country under a state of emergency since 1952, the drama still jolts me.

Up to now it has been a Friday of triple pleasure. I have just received a full month's salary with three months arrears as an untrained teacher at Kahũgũinĩ Primary School in Gatũndũ, where I had started in January, a month after I left Alliance. I have been getting a percentage of the wages pending results of the Overseas Cambridge School Certificate exams, which I took in December. It may not be much, even with the four months arrears, but fifty pounds is the largest amount of money I have ever held in my hands.

With some of it, I am able to transform my wardrobe. This is important for a new self. At Alliance, trousers were not allowed. Even shoes were for Saturdays and Sundays only. The school did not want clothes to reflect and deepen social difference. The rule was fine for me because I could not have afforded the extra expense. But after leaving school I wanted to mark the difference between the Alliance and after-Alliance lifestyle, the way I had seen my predecessors do.

Earlier today I asked Kenneth to accompany me to an Indian tailor where sometime back I had ordered made-to-measure gray woolen trousers. It was gabardine or worsted wool, the shopkeeper had explained. Very expensive. At the time, I could only afford a down payment, with the rest to be paid in monthly installments. Now with my full salary plus arrears, I was able to pay the remaining amount. I could hardly wait to change into the new pair of woolen trousers and put my old pair in a box. When I did, I walked around in the shop, looking every inch a college-bound student. Even Kenneth, who was used to wearing trousers of reasonable quality since he had started earning earlier, was impressed and ordered his own made to measure.

In addition to the full wage and new clothes, two other items of news have added to the value of this Friday. I have passed the Overseas Cambridge School Certificate, with Distinctions, in English language, history, physics with chemistry, and biology, second only to Henry Chasia. I have also clocked a credit in additional math. In my bag, I have acceptance papers to Makerere University College, one of nineteen admissions from Alliance. I brought them all to the headquarters in Kĩambu as proof of having passed the exams, the condition for securing my arrears, but I also take pride in having them with me. Throughout the morning, among the throng of teachers old and new who, as usual, have traveled from all over the district to the headquarters to receive their salaries, I have felt like waving the papers to everybody to see that I am a graduate of Alliance and a prospective college student. But I have not done so. I want to share the news with my mother first. It's the result of our pact, made twelve years ago.

58

So eager was I to get home that, in Nairobi, I rejected entreaties from Kenneth and Patrick to while away the time in the city and take a later Nairobi-Limuru bus. The anticipation of the smile on my mother's face as I place the money and papers on her lap would not let me stay. And now this delay at Banana Hills!

It is irritating. Inconvenient. Otherwise I do not see how it should concern me. I never leave my passbook behind; it tells my status as a student. Of course, I have left Alliance, but fortunately I have the admission papers to Makerere in July. Passengers without passbooks or tax receipts or identity papers are hounded out of the bus, where other officers order them to squat in twos at the roadside. The acts are repetitive, other people's boring business, and I resume my reveries.

A slap on the shoulder and a bellowing voice startle me. I look up, only to see the face of growling Mr. Rifleman.

Are you drunk or what? Show me your tax papers.

I'm a student, I say. I have just left school. Alliance High School, I add, to make an impression.

Is this the route to Alliance?

No, I am going home. Limuru.

Where are you coming from? School?

Kahũgũinĩ. Gatũndũ.

Gatũndũ? Is that not Jomo Kenyatta's home?

Kahũgũinĩ is not Gatũndũ, I say, half a truth.

Are you a Kenyatta follower?

I am a student, I answer vaguely.

Is Alliance at Kahũgũinĩ?

No. It is at Kikuyu. Carey Francis, you know, the mathematician, is the principal.

So Carey Francis told you not to pay poll tax?

No. I am just a student.

And what were you doing at Kenyatta's place?

Kahũgũinĩ! I say to clarify the distinction. I explain that I have secured a temporary position pending exam results—

Mr. Rifleman interrupts me. Oh, so you are a teacher. And I take it that you don't teach for free, or do you?

No, but—

Don't play games with me. Show me your tax receipts.

I don't have any. Look at these papers. I am going to Makerere. Uganda. In July! First-year university student.

He laughs loudly. By now all the passengers are focused on us. He is performing for them. He calls out to the other policeman, Mr. Machine Gun. Come and see who says that he is an Alliance prince bound for Makerere to meet with the Kabaka, the king of Buganda, too important to pay taxes. He continues waving the papers, which he has not bothered to read. I should not have mentioned Alliance, Makerere, or Uganda.

Are you saying that you are more educated than Dr. Julius Kĩano?

I try to ignore the sarcasm. No, I say.

Then listen. Even Julius Kĩano, Tom Mboya, and Oginga Odinga* pay taxes, he says, thrusting the papers back to me and ordering me to get out, literally pulling me from my seat and shoving me along the aisle. Not to be outdone by Mr. Rifleman, Mr. Machine Gun pushes me to the ground, where another policeman directs me to the back of the line of captives. There must have been other victims from earlier buses because the line is quite long.

I still harbor hope that the misunderstanding will be cleared up, that they will realize that in mentioning Alliance and Makerere, I was not trying to show that I am more important than any other person, and they will let me back onto the bus. But then the bus leaves. With a sinking heart, I watch it disappear in the distance. Soon afterward, the roadblock is also dismantled, and Messrs. Rifleman and

---

* The three were prominent members of the African Elected Members Organization (AEMO).

Machine Gun leave in a jeep. We are still guarded by others, also armed with rifles, but these are underlings and they either don't or won't tell us the next step. This is so absurd. I have a lot of money in my pocket, I have Makerere papers, I won't see my mother tonight, and nobody at home knows my fate.

And then at that moment, another bus from Nairobi arrives and stops by the scene. Curious about the long line of squatters, the passengers peer through the windows. Among them are Kenneth and Patrick. They come out of the bus and ask what the matter is, but our guards just shrug their shoulders. What do they want to do with the captives? *Shauri ya Wakubwa*, they say, but they do allow me to speak to Kenneth. I give him most of the money and my parcel of old clothes to take to my mother. Their bus also leaves, but now I have the comfort of knowing that somebody will take the news of my arrest to my family. My mother will get some of the money all right, but that is not how I envisioned the scene.

They keep us in the sun till the last bus has gone. They have allowed us to sit instead of squatting, and I am grateful for this small mercy. My worries deepen. It is not only the uncertainty of what next. Even if released, I will now not know what to do, where to spend the night, or how to walk the twenty kilometers to Limuru. I know that my auntie Kabera is married and lives around Banana Hills, but I don't know the actual location of her homestead. I am in limbo. The absurdity of my situation increases. Trying to make sense of it all, I retrace the events of the day.

In the morning, at Kahũgũinĩ, I was the revered teacher. Teaching had not been my first choice, even as a temporary post, pending acceptance to college. I had really wanted to be a journalist, and when the editor of the *East African Standard,* the only major English daily in Kenya, conducted interviews at Alliance, I had presented myself, but I was not successful. Once I started, however, I developed a feeling for teaching and forgot all about my journalistic ambition. I felt a rapport with my students. The headmaster, Kĩmani Ware, who pronounced his last name as if it were the English word of the same spelling, was given to dramatics, and within weeks of my joining the school, everybody in the region knew that an Alliance genius was on his staff. When the results of the Cambridge exams were printed in the *East African Standard,* Kĩmani Ware would carry the page with him as evidence of the genius on his staff.

This morning we traveled from Kahũgũinĩ to Kĩambu together, and later, after we received our pay, he had urged me to go back with him to Thika and Kahũgũinĩ, offering to accompany me to Limuru the following day. But I had declined: I had to go home to my mother to celebrate the success of our pact.

Now I am here on a roadside, not knowing what is going to happen next.

The jeep that took Messrs. Rifleman and Machine Gun returns eventually; the officers whisper something to our guards, and then leave. A decision at last, but not in our favor. They shove us into a line of twos and escort us to Thĩmbĩgwa home guard post. The post consists of a main building of stone walls and iron roof next to a few others of timber around an open yard. A fence of barbed wire surrounds the entire compound. We are crowded into a room with hardly any light. All the other rooms in the barrack are full. There must have been a general sweep; our bus was the last into the net. If only I had heeded the voices of Kenneth and Patrick or even that of Kĩmani Ware, I would not have been caught in the dragnet. I don't want to wallow in self-pity, but I cannot comprehend the turn of events from hope in the morning to despair in the evening.

And then a sudden break in the rhythm. Good Wallace and my half-brother Joseph Kabae come to visit. I feel tears at the edges of my eyes. Kenneth has obviously passed on the news.

59

Whenever I now think of Good Wallace, the image of us talking to each other, a wall of barbed wire between us at Ngenia, pops up, but this is quickly offset by the other of him at home, a family reunion again after his ordeals in the mountains and concentration camp. We realized how narrowly he had escaped harm when, in March, news splashed across the world about the massacre of eleven political inmates at Hola Camp. Dubbed hardcore for continually resisting, they had been bludgeoned to death. The Horror at Hola suddenly alerted the world to the reality Kenyans had been enduring for seven years since the declaration of a state of emergency in 1952. Even from the hallowed halls of Westminster, Labour MPs demanded an answer from Harold Macmillan. After all, Kenya was still a British colony. On Good Wallace's release, though, he had told us that he had been lucky, that throughout his stay in the camps, he never faced a situation like the Horror at Hola.

Good Wallace never ceased to amaze me. On his release late in 1957, he had reinvented himself from a former carpenter, guerrilla fighter, and war prisoner to a market trader, buying and selling foodstuff and managing to float just above the water. He refused to bow down to hardship. And now, only a few months after, he is here, for me, with Joseph Kabae. I note that Good Wallace stays a step behind Kabae, who does all the talking. Even in civilian clothes, Kabae has never lost his military bearing, a remnant of his days as a member of the King's African Rifles, during World War II. His chain smoking, crushing the cigarette ends under his shoes slowly and deliberately or flinging them away expertly, gives him an air of authority. Used to command, he has no difficulties in inducing subservience and getting permission to speak to me. They let me step out; Kabae keeps the guards in conversation to buy Good Wallace and me time to talk. He quickly tells me a few more details of the day he left the mountains and gave himself up to Chief Karŭga.

Good Wallace tells me that on the eve of his presenting himself at Karŭga's house, he had slept, cold and hungry and all alone, under coffee bushes not far from here, not knowing whether, if caught, he would be shot dead on the spot or be sent to the gallows at Gĩthũngũri. He is trying to encourage me to keep hope alive. He assures me that Kabae will use his contacts in government to secure my release. His mention of cold and hunger has awakened my stomach. They will bring me some food, he tells me, which they do: a loaf of bread, shortly after. Kabae reiterates that I have not broken any law; he will ensure my release. The guards he talked to were underlings with no authority to do anything about the inmates, so negotiations for my release will have to await the new day.

As I watch them leave, the irony does not escape me. Not so long ago, they were on the inside and I on the outside, gazing helplessly at their brotherly dance of death, with Kabae on the government's side and Wallace in the mountains. The glow of the spirits I felt in their presence wanes. But they have assured me of release: it is matter of enduring the night.

60

We are massed together, standing room only, in the dark. I don't know what to do about the toilet. I follow what I have seen others do: shout for permission to go to the toilet outside, under a guard. My voice is too weak, and the others express solidarity by hollering to the guard for me. My bladder relieved, I am back inside, standing again. No, it's too much for my feet; I push my way to a corner, slide to the floor, and sit, my back against the wall.

By now word has spread that among the inmates is a captive from Alliance. They turn to me, ghostly voices in the dark, curious. To their questions, I can only say, I don't know, tears in my eyes, occasioned by their pity. I may be the youngest among them, but I must not succumb to tears, not even silent sobs. I can hold back only by remaining deaf to even the most insistent whispers of sympathy. I retreat into myself. Would it have helped if, in the bus, I had kept quiet about being a college-bound graduate of Alliance? I doubt it. I feel like I have gone through this before, that what is happening to me fits into a pattern that has dogged my path since that January afternoon four years ago, when the gates of Alliance opened and I entered. I recall my return to Limuru after my first term to find my old homestead a wasteland.

The sage who once said that the events of history appear twice, first as tragedy and then as farce, could have been talking about my current situation. Thĩmbĩgwa post, where I am now held, could have been a replica of the community prison I helped to build four years back. The shock of that first return had the ring of tragedy. The present is a comedy without laughter. What can top this absurdity of my being held in a garrison for nothing more criminal than stating that I have been to Alliance?

Wrestling with these memories has neither helped numb the pain I feel nor blunted the humiliation. After ten there is no going outside for relief. Darkness hides the identity of those who use the walls to ease pressed bladders. But it does not cover up the stench. My mother used to tell us that even the longest night ends with dawn. I cling to the hope that in the morning I will leave this stench behind me.

61

SATURDAY

A bugle accompanying the raising of the Union Jack interrupts the restless stream of images in my mind. I hope that this day will be kinder and gentler than yesterday. As if in response, dawn brings back Good Wallace, Kabae, and a loaf of bread. The inmates depend on relatives to bring them food. Those without anybody who knows their whereabouts depend on what they can get from the others. I break the bread with those near me.

Kabae is at his impressive best, with curls of smoke issuing from his mouth and crushed cigarette ends under his boots. The guards are apologetic as they explain that their white boss is not yet in but will definitely appear. As they leave, promising to return later in the morning, Good Wallace tells me that they worked through the night and contacted important people, by which I understand that they bribed those who claimed to have influence. Kabae assures me that something good will happen today.

The white district officer, who apparently does not spend nights in the post, finally drives in. Perhaps this is a testament to Kabae's power and influence. Life visibly stirs all around. The police stand at attention, saluting their boss, calling him *effendi,* in what amounts to a visual absurdity. The officers are tall, big, older, armed. Their boyish boss is shorter, thinner, and civilian clad, looking harmless except for the pistol hanging from his hip, which he keeps touching as if he is afraid of his own officers. The inmates reiterate to each other for the umpteenth time their innocence and certainty of release once the white officer hears the truth. Whites are more understanding than their black underlings, a case of the kindly master who does not know that his ferocious dogs have their fangs open at innocents.

One at a time, the inmates go into the office and then come back into custody in the same order with the same complaint: the officer listens only to the policeman, his sole informant, translator, and interpreter. There is no more talk of the difference between the master at home and his dog at the gate. They are the same colonial shit.

Eventually, it is my turn into the office. The officer is playing stern and serious, probably to impress his authority on his much-older African underlings. Even the way he bends forward over an open file, holding a pen, seems a performance to impress an audience, a behavior almost identical to that of Johnny the Green, three years ago. Without looking up, he asks why I did not pay taxes. Having heard what those before me said about the police interpreter, I hasten to speak for myself. I recently left school, I answer him in English. I have papers to prove it, I add quickly, not to give space for the interpreter to intervene. A pause, a slight pause, then with his eyes still bent over the file, he stretches his hand for the documents. I give him my college admission papers, which include my performance on the Cambridge exams. He studies them intently, and now he looks up at me. Do I detect surprise on his face? A blush even? His name suggests itself: Johnny the Red.

Alliance?

Yes.

Bound for college, I see?

Yes.

Johnny the Red leans back, seemingly relaxed, as if ready to hold a conversation on a theme more to his taste than the sordid business of probing if poor farmers, men older than him, have paid taxes or are telling the truth.

You have beaten me to it, he says, with something like a smile. I am waiting to hear if I have been accepted at Oxford. I am a graduate of Duke of York, your nemesis in hockey, he adds with a hint of pride.

The conversation I had with Andrew Brockett a year ago in Mutonguini flashes across my mind. The young officer sitting in judgment over my fate is waiting to go to college? His job in government, like mine at Kahũgũinĩ, is temporary. Our situations are similar. But we are on opposite sides of the table, a gun between us, I remind myself, as I listen to him. He is still into sports. He can remember the last victorious hockey engagement with Alliance. He was a member of the team, he says, and I congratulate him as if the victory has just occurred. I want to remind him that last November in four soccer engagements, two home and two away, Alliance beat York, but I don't think I should be reminding him of defeat. I simply add that indeed York is better than both

Alliance and Wales in hockey, which puts him in an even better mood, to the continued chagrin and incomprehension of the police interpreter. All because of sports, I am thinking, still anxious and uncertain about my fate. Finally he asks me what I have been doing since I left Alliance. I tell him. As far as I can see, your papers are in order, he says handing them back to me. You can go, he continues almost wearily.

I am also weary but elated as I leave the premises. On the way out, I see one of the arresting officers, Mr. Rifleman, head toward the room hurriedly. I ignore him and wave to my fellow inmates. I don't look back. I am already in transition from incarceration to celebration, hoping that I might meet with my brothers and save them from having to come all this way for nothing. Their mission has been accomplished.

I am about to round the corner and vanish when I hear footsteps behind me. It is the police interpreter. He stops me. Bwana officer wants you, he tells me.

Maybe I have left one of my papers behind, I think as I walk back, the policeman behind me. One glance at the erstwhile gentleman, and I know that his mood has changed. Johnny the Red, the hockey-loving-college-student-in-waiting has resumed his authoritarian look of a British colonial officer determined to enforce law and order. He has found something more morally uplifting to enforce than chasing poor farmers for poll tax.

So you were resisting arrest? Even fighting my own officers? Do you think that Alliance has given you license to attack a police officer doing his duty? He does not let me explain. Take him back to his kind, he orders. Mr. Rifleman is still in the room, actually standing by the side of his young boss, and I can see a triumphant glint in his eyes.

Nobody earns the young officer's clemency. New, inexperienced, with little knowledge of the laws he is enforcing, he relies almost wholly on the words of the police, who have been in the field many more years.

In the evening, the police huddle us into a truck. Under armed escort, the truck leaves the precinct. They don't tell us where we are headed. For all I know, they may be taking us to a quarry to open fire on us. Throughout the state of emergency, I have heard of people detained on whatever suspicions, released in a forest and told they were free to go home, then shot in the back as terrorists in a running battle. It is only when the truck stops by a barbed-wire fence and the gates open to swallow us that I know from the others that we are in Kĩambu Remand Prison.

Talk of comedy! Yesterday, Friday, I was here in Kĩambu to collect the largest wages of my life. I was with friends. Now I am back in the same town, without the money, and nobody knows me. The prison guards shake their heads to every question concerning the fate that awaits us. A Saturday in ruins, I note in my mental diary.

62

On arrival at Kĩambu Remand Prison, we are made to stand in line and take out whatever valuables we have—money, watches, and other personal items—and hand them over to reception, where they are counted, recorded, and put in different bags that are labeled and put aside behind the counter. We are distributed among strangers to different rooms, already holding other inmates awaiting trial. It feels like a family separation. So when three of us from Thĩmbĩgwa are pushed into one cell, I feel lucky. They lock the door from the outside.

A few minutes later they open it and throw in some blankets, and we grab whatever we can lay our hands on. We sit on the cold cement floor, our bodies almost touching, blankets wrapped around our feet and knees. The room, designed for four, now holds eight. An electric bulb deep in the ceiling lights up the room, but not too well. Soon we get used to it and are able to see a clearer outline of each other.

The inmates already in our room could be my age, but their faces are hardened. They look at us warily as if we are intruding into their home. Two of the Thĩmbĩgwans are clearly elderly, at least compared with the rest of us. For some time, the earlier inmates only murmur among themselves, but the inevitable questions about why we have been brought here eventually break the barrier between the old and the new. I don't participate, but one of the Thĩmbĩgwans reveals that I am from Alliance. They all shake their heads, murmuring disapproval as if my arrest, so obviously wrong, proves that they too have been held by mistake. It's the evil character of the colonial police. This state of emergency has given them the license to do whatever they want. They don't want to see us black people educated.

The shared sympathy for my position triggers stories of why they left school—tuition, failed tests, cruel teachers, or simply the lure of a more exciting life, which they now admit was an illusion. One or two have never been inside a classroom: there were no schools in their area, the independent ones having been banned.

How then did they end up here? One was arrested after snatching a wallet from an Indian woman; another trying to break into a drapery to steal. Others tried to rob a bank with a gun rented from a police officer for a share of the loot. They feel betrayed: the insider on whose information they had relied was a plant. When they finally catch up with the traitor, no matter how long it takes, they will exact vengeance. There's no emotion; it's a statement, chilling because it carries a certainty of intention. More chilling for me, a revelation, is this partnership in crime between criminals and crime busters.

For some, their present arrest is just one more in a series that has already seen them in and out of prison: crime has become a way of life. Others exchange their experiences in different prisons at different times. A few tell of how time and again they managed to talk their way out of the gallows into a prison term, which they served with exemplary behavior that earned them remission.

These tell of their experiences, not in pride or resignation, but matter-of-factly, as one might talk about meeting an unexpected mishap during a leisurely stroll down the street. They don't complain about the conditions that drove them to their ways; they are not judgmental about the social conditions that have shaped their lives; they take society the way they take the reality of physical nature and its vagaries. You do what you have to do to live with it, not to change it, for how does one change the reality of mountains, rivers, floods, fires?

63

I notice that my fellow Thĩmbĩgwans have become increasingly quiet, almost as if they recognize the differences between their experiences and those of the young men. They are older; they seem surprised that here in the remand prison are people who own up to crimes and discuss their involvement calmly. In their own case, they were victims of the administrative police who were looking for the slightest reason, even a manufactured one, to make arrests.

The situation changes when one of the self-confessed criminals brags about the courage involved in the deeds they do. Even pickpocketing involves observance, quick hands and feet, and steady nerves. One of the Thĩmbĩgwans eventually breaks his silence. He speaks slowly, almost in a whisper.

Young men, I will speak to you because you could be any of my sons, and fate has now brought us together. There is no courage in snatching people's wallets, be they European, Asian, or African. There is no courage in renting a gun from a policeman to risk your life so that the man supposed to enforce the law can dispose of the loot however he likes. Courage is in those young men and women who took to the mountains to face an enemy armed ten times more than they, not for their individual gains, but because they were responding to the cries of a community. Courage, my sons, is in the old man Mbiyũ, who gave up the glories of a senior chief and the wealth of a big landowner and the peace of old age, to throw in his lot with the community.

Are you talking of ex-senior chief Koinange wa Mbiyũ? asks the bank robber, or Mr. Bank Robber, as the name etches itself in my mind. What has he given up, his land? My grandfather worked for him for many years, and did he give him a piece of the lands he owns? His sons are safe in England; another is a chief even now . . .

He cannot be expected to give a piece of land to every landless person in the country and leave the whites to sit on lands they stole from us. His sons have not escaped persecution. What additions to his wealth was he after? No, it was for all of us, the landless, the poor. Because of his agitation for education, land, and freedom for all, the old man languishes in a remote desert place, Marsabit.

Yes, but I hear he has all the servants he needs, and even his wives are allowed to live with him.

In exile? Marsabit? Banished from his home and family? Wouldn't you rather be in your home without servants than live in Hell with servants to look after your burns?

What has he sacrificed really? Where is the courage?

It has become a two-person war, of words, yes, but a war all the same. The elderly man keeps quiet for a while, as if he has decided not to continue, but he is only reorganizing his thoughts for defense and assault.

The old man has given the ultimate in self-sacrifice for a cause bigger than himself. I will say this here, and if anybody should carry the words out of this circle, I will deny everything, to my grave.

He draws a portrait of the old man, from the 1920s onward: his being appointed a colonial chief and then turning the title into a platform for airing anticolonial grievances; his struggle for education for all, though he never went to school; his testimony to the Carter Land Commission in London; his turning his home in Kīambaa into a parliament where many nationalists gathered to plan for our freedom.

He tells a gripping story of how the war for freedom was planned in the old chief's homestead; how he had turned one of his hidden stores into an armory; how very few knew of the actual secret place. But somehow Gathiomi, one of his sons, discovered it. The decision was taken to disappear him. It was his life or that of thousands. Confronted with the choice, the old man did not say no. Young man, do you read the Bible? Do you know how Abraham felt when asked to sacrifice his son for a greater cause? Only in his case, God intervened and provided an alternative. The same book gives us another example. *For God so loved the world, that he gave his only begotten Son . . .* Well, Gathiomi was not his only son, but a father loves all his children equally.

As a boy growing up in Limuru, I had heard whispers

about the mystery of Gathiomi's disappearance. Now the incident is being discussed openly in the most unlikely of places, ten years later, within two or so miles of the old chief's homestead. A razor could have cut the tension in the room, a cough from one of the other Thĩmbĩgwans only intensifying it.

And what courage, other than evading tax collectors, do you have to show? Mr. Bank Robber asks, rather sarcastically.

Here we are all strangers, and yet they are going at it as if they were old adversaries.

Young man, he says, not paying taxes to a cruel government is not the worst of crimes. But I pay all the same to avoid this kind of thing. It takes me away from my work. I did not have the papers on me at the time, and these dogs would not listen to any explanation. As for courage, well, let me tell you, I may not be able to hold a knife or fire a gun, but—

He stops, chokingly. When he resumes, he tells a most incredible story. He sees himself as a freedom fighter. He used to work in Nairobi. Once a very cruel area assistant chief, who had killed many patriots with his own hands, was captured and sentenced to death by a people's court. How were they going to get rid of his body? The colonial forces would turn everything upside down. So the executioners cut him into pieces. Then people, among them the storyteller, were each given a piece to bury, in the rural areas outside Nairobi. The people did not know the executioners or any of the other carriers. The idea was that nobody should have all the information, in case caught and tortured. The storyteller was given his piece—an arm. He wrapped it in paper, put it in a basket, and rode a bus. Just outside Nairobi the bus was stopped. The police entered and even poked at his package. He was sweating. The package oozed blood. But the police were more interested in those who did not have their papers in order. The memory of the encounter and narrow escape overwhelms him. Even his verbal adversary holds back his tongue.

You see the irony? Yesterday I was coming from the field, and now I am here. Why? Because my papers were not in order.

Total silence follows. His name forms in my mind: Mr. Body Parts. Although I can't see the faces of the other prisoners clearly, it appears to me that there is a change in how they look at him. There is now a hint of awe or fear. I feel the chill myself: I would not want to brush against him. Why did he tell us his story? Does prison create a space for confessions? Is it because the listeners are total strangers, not likely to repeat it? Or is it the closeness of shared grievance? I don't know. I recall that when I was once in the hospital, patients tended to talk their hearts out to each other. But I also note that in all the conversation today, nobody gives their names or any details of their homes and family. I am the only one with a known location: Alliance.

64

Suddenly the two robbers and a third inmate make signs to each other. They stand up and come toward me. I am terrified. But they just want to go to the doorless toilet hole, at the corner in the same room. Two of them hold the edges of a blanket to make a curtain at the entrance; the third person goes behind the curtain, and soon I hear the sound of his bowels. They do it in turns. I am overwhelmed by the stink. I feel like throwing up, but I have nothing to let out. After several hours I stop smelling it and then realize that it is only because everybody and everything smells the same. I find it striking, amusing even, that these who have confessed to terrible deeds still maintain a sense of modesty when it comes to shitting.

I want and don't want to sleep. I am wary of the warders outside, my fellow inmates, the room, everything. There is no escape, no retreat even; I am bound to their company. I'm privy to their secrets. They have not been hostile to me, by word or gesture. But their stories have stirred inside me a fear I cannot define. When I start dozing, I find myself fighting to remain awake, watchful, although I don't know why. But I feel it's important to keep my eyes open, open, open. It is a struggle. I end up suspended between sleep and wakefulness.

I drift into a plantation. As the wind blows, the breeze turns the surface, as though opening the pages of a book, to reveal different crops—coffee, tea, sisal, cotton—that extend to the horizon on all sides. I am the only worker in this vast plantation. If I try to rest, a bank-robber-turned-overseer prevents me. In one hand he holds a huge machete; in the other a *sjambok,* which he cracks every time I show slackness. Why, why? He is black like me. Then from nowhere appears his master on a horse whose hooves are made of rubber. If he slacks again, he tells the bank robber, pointing at me, cut him up into pieces. I want to protest, but no words issue from my mouth. I try harder. Instead of bare words, out comes a melody, *My Lord what a morning,* at first hoarsely, as if a cough is stuck in my throat, and then smoothly:

> You'll hear the trumpet sound to wake the nations under-
> ground,
> Looking to my God's right hand, when the stars begin to fall.

I look up at the vast canopy above, and I see only one star, whose light is masked by gray and dark clouds. The master gallops away to escape the impending rain. Is this a signal for the overseer to start cutting me up? Then from nowhere I see men in blankets wrapped around their waists, their upper torsos bare, walking toward me slowly, singing, *Swing low, sweet chariot,* but ending with the line, *coming for to carry you home.*

No, no, they cannot deceive me. I know the home they are talking about. Each has been ordered to carry a piece of me hidden in their blankets to bury it in remote parts of the plantation. At first I plead with them to be aware of the overseer: I know the orders that the owner has given him; once he finishes with me, he will do the same to each of you. They don't heed my words, so I sing back, drowning their voices with my one voice that calls out: *Freedom, oh freedom.* Now they hear me. We join voices:

And before I'll be a slave
I'll be buried in my grave
And go home to my Lord and be free.

It is not the burial in the grave part of it that moves me but rather its reiteration of *Freedom! Freedom! Oh freedom over me.* I find so much power in its categorical assertion of *no more moaning* and its promise of space for singing and praying, for what am I doing but praying for a day without a landlord and an overseer on my back? Looking from side to side and back again in terror, the overseer starts retreating, his huge machete and *sjambok* somehow merging into a rifle in front of our eyes.

Still, we go after him, defiantly singing *Ain't gonna let nobody turn me 'roun'. I say I'm gonna hold out until my change comes,* waving our blankets in the air, like flags. The strength in numbers has made all the difference.

65

The noise of shit and piss jolts me back to reality. The choristers are simply my fellow inmates queuing to visit the hole. The toilet is full, overflowing, and even the brave ones curse as, behind the blanket of modesty, they make more deposit of shit and urine.

I cling to my corner for all it is worth. Let me retreat deeper into self, the way I did the night before at Thĩmbĩgwa, pretend that I am here, in this inferno, for one night only. But I must not slide back to sleep. It is difficult: competing images flit across the void. I must select an image of something good that has happened to me in the past and hold on to it, like that of the day the doors of Alliance opened, that January four years ago. Instead, here comes the district officer, a boy my age, a leering smile on his face, reminding me that earlier in the day he let me go, only to bring me back to him, a white cat playing with a black mouse. He has stolen into my dreams disguised as a plantation owner. Everything about him is disguise. But this time he cannot deceive me. I am not a mouse; I am human. I have done no wrong. What does the white boy have that I don't? With malicious glee, my only triumph over him, I think of him as having failed in his bid for college. And even physically, one on one, blow for blow, I think I could hold my own: was I not once circumcised into manhood? Yes, a voice answers me, but this has nothing to do with manhood, age, physique, or mind:

do you want to know the great image of authority? Yes, I answer back. He has vanished. Just like that. Instead I hear Andrew Kaingu's voice, speaking lines from *King Lear:*

Thou hast seen a farmer's dog bark at a beggar?
And the creature run from the cur?

Yes, yes, Lord Kahahu's dog once made me take flight. It bit me. What did you do? the voice asks. Nothing, just went home crying. The voice laughs and says, *a dog's obeyed in office.*

But I refuse to obey. As if in response to my defiance, the white boy reappears in a Land Rover full of armed soldiers and banishes me to Marsabit. I am adorned in a toga of Colobus monkey skin. I find others in similar wear. We are all men of some means, evidenced by the rare animal skins we wear. Marsabit is a forest of green cacti that sprout big leaves and flowers where there should be thorns. Marsabit is a cover name for arcadia, where the exile finds a home and the weary traveler, peace. Here in the Marsabit arcadia, leaf-lets, pinned on tree trunks, carry messages of love. But wait, it is all an illusion. It's the RAF dropping bombs on us, which turn into harmless leaflets as they reach the ground. I pick one up. It warns us that we shall be cut up in small pieces unless we come out of the forest. We run through the trees, in different directions. I wander through the forest in a tattered blanket, alone. It is raining, and the wind is howl-ing. A small man appears from nowhere and runs a straw through my tattered garments, and I can only cry out helplessly: it is unfair; this is not justice. And the small man is saying, Look, it is all an illusion, it is not raining, the sun is shining over a field of lilies. I sit down on a fallen tree trunk: it is indeed shining. The small man is talking to me about a journey's end:

> Think but this, and all is mended,
> That you have but slumber'd here
> While these visions did appear.
> And this weak and idle theme,
> No more yielding but a dream.

A dream! Dreams within dreams! What a relief, I murmur to myself as I wake up to sun's rays streaming through the open door and the tiny windows. The prison warders are saying: out, out, stand in twos for your porridge. It is Sunday morning.

66

SUNDAY

I turn over the images of my prison night's dream. I have always tried to make sense of the apparent illogicality of events in dreams. The images are often drawn from what has happened in the day or earlier in time. The illogical lies in the way these images are linked. Sometimes I fear when this happens to me in daytime. What does one call it when, in the fields or walking alone, different images begin to link up? What about when flowers in a field suddenly begin to dance in front of you or birds talk to you? Or a person walking in front of you is transformed into another person, from another place, another time? Is that also a dream?

But I should not have been surprised that images from spirituals should come to me in prison at night. Not too long ago, with my Kahũgũinĩ students, I had organized a performance, similar to the one I had done with the Limuru youth, at Kamandũra. This time the spirituals and other hymns centered on the theme of sacrifice, connecting Abraham's intended sacrifice of Isaac to the actual sacrifice of Jesus on the Cross. Through dance and song, we told of barren Sarah pleading to God and then hearing His response through an angel. She gets a laughing boy she calls Isaac. We made a few additions to the biblical story, and eventually, again through dance and song, Sarah is transformed into Mary, crying for her only child, crucified. She too hears a voice that talks of resurrection into new life. There was no script: it was an oral improvisation, a thin fictional story line linking the two biblical events. The main performance was in a church in Gatũndũ, a few weeks before my arrest.

The success was such that the elders had asked me if I could have repeat performances. Kĩmani Ware was for it, as it meant Kahũgũinĩ Primary School continually being the talk of the community. With my Cambridge results and admission to Makerere, I knew that I had only a few weeks left. A farewell performance was clearly in order. I was to give a definite answer this very Sunday.

67

Despite my doubts about evangelism, I had somehow maintained an internal facade. Even without a confessional support group, I still clung to my faith, however riddled with doubt. Kĩmani Ware and my fellow teachers at Kahũgũinĩ tried to tempt me with alcohol and women. I decided to wear my faith on my sleeve. I would preach to them occasionally, which bolstered my resistance and dampened their enjoyment of sin. Even when I kept mum, they felt the moral weight of my silent presence. The more they tested me, the surer I felt about my faith. This was no consolation, for I was not able to make them follow my path. The fact that even in my heyday as a Balokole, I did not manage to convert anybody, had always deepened my unease about the conviction with which I stated my religious beliefs. As if they sensed this, my fellow teachers amused themselves by arguing back and asking questions for which I had no answer. How come Christians condemned polygamy yet believed in a Bible that featured Solomon of a hundred wives? Or Abraham impregnating his maid, Hagar, and then driving her and her son Ishmael into the desert?

These were not questions that seriously troubled them. They were asking just to hear me answer back. They were all nominally Christian. Why do you go to church every Sunday? I would ask, trying to turn tables around. They had no problem in saying that they went there to worship and pray to God. And how do you end your prayers? In the name of Jesus Christ, Amen. See, you profess to be Christians and then deny it. Yes, but we are not the *twakutendereza Yesu,* the Saved, like you. That would bring a truce, but temporary only.

They were otherwise very nice to me, receiving me in their homes, and our talk was not all religion. One of the teachers said that there was a lady teacher in his village in the Ng'enda area who devoured books, including the Bible: no man was a match for her in brains and no woman, in beauty. It would be interesting, he said, for she and I to meet. I laughed the matter off. Outside debates, I was never interested in intellectual contests for the sake of contest. I liked discussions and exchanges of ideas and experiences. I believed that there was always something to learn from every encounter.

One weekend this teacher invited me to his home. I was particularly well received, with what amounted to a small banquet of roasted goat meat and *irio*. His one-bedroom was packed with young men and women my age, who were happy to be in the company of an Alliance graduate. I sat on the bed. My host, like the others, had exaggerated my learning and my performance at Alliance, claiming that some of the teachers there used to consult me when they failed to solve a problem. So they had come to see a genius in the flesh. I felt relaxed but inevitably questions of faith arose. Should I ruin this cozy atmosphere with morality? But the girls would not leave me alone: they wanted to know if I was really saved. Pushed into a corner, I said yes, firmly.

And then, just after the food had been cleared, the lantern throwing agitated shadows on the wall, she entered, like an actor entering the stage on cue. We shall call her Lady Teacher. All eyes were turned to her as she sat on a chair vacated for her. She was treated like a challenger to a reigning champion in a boxing ring. The talk resumed. At first the newcomer did not say much; she mostly listened, sometimes raising her big dark eyes. She was an untrained teacher in a nearby school, I learned. Was she the one I had heard so much about? Why, then, was she so silent? I could not tell if her silence was in wonder or skepticism. No matter how hard I tried, I could not get my eyes away from the light in her eyes. And then she started talking, asking questions and dissenting, gently, and I realized straight away that she had not come for a contest, that she was genuinely troubled by profound doubt.

How come a loving God allows famines and diseases, so much suffering, in the world? Why does he allow white people to kill black people? You say that God speaks to us, she said, directing the question at me. In what language does he speak to you? Does he talk to black people in their language and white people in theirs? Is he in favor of one over another?

I almost fell out of my seat. These were the same questions I had asked E.K. I could not admit that God did not speak to me in a discernible language. I resorted to the primacy of faith. God speaks directly to the heart, without the medium of a specific language. God speaks his own language. I wrapped myself in faith. Then what is the point of using reason to explain matters of faith? And why is one faith more believable than another? I recommended some passages from the Bible, but she knew them already, plus many other passages and incidents that contradicted the ones I had cited. By this time, we had shut out others who looked on our exchange as a contest, but for me it was like hearing echoes of an earlier conversation, within myself: what color is Jesus? And then the challenge: was God a man or a woman?

God's gender? I had never really thought of God in terms of gender. I always assumed him to be male, although in Gĩkũyũ God is neither man nor woman, he is a thing, a big it! But the color of Jesus had arisen before in my life, when Sam Ntiro and his student, Elimo Njau, visited Alliance, talked to us about art, and showed us paintings of a black Christ. Now I recalled all of that, and I was able to sincerely elaborate on God making humans in his own image. People can see God and Jesus in any color or gender. In other words, since we are made in God's image, each one of us can know what God looks like by looking deep into ourselves.

And suddenly I felt like something had been revealed to me. I had answered some of my old questions; rather, I talked as I had often talked to myself, whenever I felt uncertain about my faith. At that point even my own doubts seemed swept away, as I placed faith above reason in matters of belief. I wallowed in eloquence. I was gaining ground. The room had become silent. Here was my chance to convert one person, the challenger. I was so absorbed in my words, enjoying my anticipated evangelical triumph, that I did not notice that all the others had left the room. It was just me and the beautiful listener, whose responses were now reduced to saying, yes, yes, is that so? The paraffin lamp was losing power, making the room rather dark. Imperceptibly, still murmuring dissent and assent, the challenger had drawn nearer and now sat on the bed next to me. And when, as if reaching out for holiness, her fingers brushed against my hand, I felt the eloquence suddenly subsumed in flames.

I was surprised that I did not feel guilt. The fact that my will to resist had melted away at the first serious challenge bothered me more than a sense of sin. But I had lost any moral authority to pass quick judgment on others, I thought, recalling our holy cabal at Alliance.

I wanted to see her again. We did not meet. Two weeks later I was arrested.

68

Time in remand prison moves ever so slowly, the way the American evangelist once described the passage of time in Hell, and this Sunday will not be different. Even the process of waking up, falling in line for breakfast, receiving one's plate, eating the porridge, are in slow motion. I begin to think that this is divine retribution. The evangelist who converted me had talked of omission and commission as being equal sins. I don't want to leave things to chance. I murmur the Lord's Prayer that stuck in my throat on my first day as the new Sunday school leader at Kĩnoo. *Our*

Father who art in Heaven, hallowed be thy name, dwelling on the line, *and forgive our trespasses.* I repeat the prayer in Gĩkũyũ and Kiswahili. But no voice speaks to me directly or indirectly in any of the languages. Only silence.

The porridge has stilled my hunger. Afterward we are allowed to mingle in the yard; for those of us brought here from Thĩmbĩgwa, it feels like a family reunion. They repeat the same assertions of innocence, now spiced with complaints about conditions in our different cells. These lead to our common woe: we don't know what they want to do with us.

Some of the inmates come up with the idea of a game of checkers. Since there is no checkerboard, they draw a semblance of one in the sand. Dry bits of wood become the white pieces; green bits, the black. Kinging, or crowning, is achieved by simply doubling the sticks. People crowd around this game. Here in this place of confinement, it helps to prevent the mind from drifting into boredom, lethargy, and self-pity.

I walk to the barbed wire and look out. Kĩambu town stands on ridges with valleys in between. My eyes wander toward the location of the education headquarters, and then the Tailor's Ridge, as I call the place where I bought my customized pair of woolen trousers. I still wear them; they are my sleeping rag and cover. Remarkably, the creases have held.

From the yard, I can see people passing by on the road toward downtown Kĩambu. Members of a fundamentalist sect who wear white garments with a red cross stitched onto them follow, singing that they are on their way to Heaven. They are not walking; they are running, symbolizing their readiness. Walking without supervision seems an unreachable desire, but I long for it.

Hope rises suddenly. I see my brother, Good Wallace. I note that he is not with Kabae, whose soldierly gait and mannerism of authority so impressed the guards at Thĩmbĩgwa. I am not allowed out to see him, and he is not allowed in, but we are able to speak through the barbed wire mesh between us. I cannot forget this reversal of our positions. He is sorry that their efforts did not result in my release. He talks of his fears when yesterday he went back to Thĩmbĩgwa, and nobody could tell him where they had taken me. This morning he returned to Thĩmbĩgwa, and one police officer, after some money changed hands, told him: why don't you try Kĩambu? The same officer told him that it is likely that we will be taken to court tomorrow. He has not brought me any bread, but he excuses himself and soon rectifies the situation. My mother, he tells me, has sent a message: *Ndũgakue ngoro! Ma ndĩkuaga!* Don't give up hope! Truth never dies!

Despite his attempt to shore up my spirits, I note his helplessness. He does not try to console me with *we are seeing some people.* And he does not say a thing about Kabae and his influence. Soon the guards ask him to leave. He has a few words for me, the only thing he can give. He says: Be prepared for the worst, but always hope for the best. See you in court tomorrow. He leaves as the guards are herding us back to our cells. The hope that the court tomorrow will end my misery buoys my spirits. I whisper to one inmate what I have learned. Soon everybody has the same news about the court tomorrow.

69

MONDAY

It turns out that Monday is a public holiday. The morning porridge is tasteless. I feel as cheated as I did on Saturday, when I was rearrested minutes after being set free. I don't know how I can face the entire Monday watching my fellow inmates playing checkers over and over again with sticks for pieces and holes dug in the ground for a checkerboard. Two who try to play without spectators stop after a few moves. Everybody seems listless. I can feel their disappointment. I just hope they don't blame me for being the unwitting conduit of false hope.

I sit down, apart, then stand up and walk about, then sit down again to mull over my fate. I should not have put all my hope in a court appearance today, and I certainly should not have passed on what my brother told me.

Don't feel bad, a voice says. I look up and find Mr. Body Parts standing above me. I tense up, hoping it doesn't show. *Shauri ya Mungu*, he says, sitting beside me without invitation. God works in mysterious ways, his wonders to perform. Shall I tell you a story?

I don't feel like conversation, and I certainly hope it is not about the burial of body parts. But instead he tells me a tale of Hyena, who has fallen into a pit. He cannot climb out. He stays there, day and night, without food or water. Luckily for him, Antelope passes by and, hearing the cries of the trapped animal, stops. Hyena pleads with Antelope to get him out. Antelope stretches out his hand and helps Hyena out. Thank you very much, says Hyena, but you know what, I am very hungry, and I have to eat you. Along comes Hare, who offers to settle the dispute. They tell him what happened, and there seems to be no disagreement over the facts of the story. Hare says that he cannot believe that Hyena, so big an animal, could have fallen into such a pit. Hyena is angry at not being believed. Show me how, says Hare. When Hyena is back in the pit, Hare tells Antelope, case closed. Go your way.

He deserves it, the stupid Hyena, some voices say, and I realize that the story has attracted other listeners. There is animated talk about Hare and his cunning ways. But Hare is no match for Chameleon, another person chimes in. Without an invitation, he too tells a story.

As far as I can tell, it is a retelling of the Tortoise and the Hare, except instead of Tortoise, it is Chameleon who challenges Hare to a race. They agree to meet by a certain bush where Chameleon lives. When Hare turns up at the bush, he does not see Chameleon and waits for a few minutes. That Chameleon has chickened out, says Hare, whereupon he hears Chameleon's voice tell him, Let's start. Hare dashes ahead, and then stops, looks back. Chameleon is nowhere in sight. Even if I give him a day, he will never catch up with me, Hare says, and enters a restaurant. Our

storyteller describes the food, which in variety, color, rich-
ness, and quantity is the exact opposite of the porridge we
have been given. Hare's other stops include a night in a
whorehouse, where the room, the bed, and the bedding are
the exact opposite of ours at the remand prison. After days
of self-indulgence, Hare arrives at the agreed-upon spot. As
he sits down, he hears Chameleon's voice: Don't sit on me,
I have been waiting for you for a day and a half. What happened? asks one listener. He is asking for the sake of saying
something, because they all know the answer: Chameleon
climbed onto Hare's tail, and wherever Hare went, Chameleon changed colors accordingly and hung on, waiting for
his chance.

Did you know that it was the same two animals that
brought death to the world? asks another listener. By this
time, nearly all the inmates have become a participatory
audience, in what has turned out to be a storytelling session.
When all attention is turned to the new voice, he coughs
and tells his story of how death came to the world.

When God first created humans, he had not made up
his mind whether to make them immortal. One day he
decides that humans, because they are made in his image,
will never die. He sends Chameleon to take the good news
to the human race. It takes Chameleon many days to reach
the humans, and when he gets to them, he starts delivering
the message. Go-Go-God sa-sa-says tha-tha-that . . . In the
meantime, God has changed his mind. Because man is made
in his image, there has to be something that differentiates
the gods from the humans. Immortality for gods; mortal-

ity for humans. He dispatches Hare to tell the human race that they are mortal. Hare has to deliver his message before Chameleon's because God does not break his word. Hare arrives just as Chameleon is saying that . . . that . . . and Hare completes the sentence: humans must die.

Arguments erupt about the advantages and disadvantages of immortality. The debate shifts to qualities of different animals. More stories and anecdotes are told in support of one position or another. Even Messrs. Bank Robber and Body Parts tell more stories without flaring tempers. The stories have calmed our nerves and brought us closer together. The day passes very quickly. I recall what my mother told me about stories under the Mugumo tree.

In my corner at night, I now cling to hope. At Alliance, Carey Francis used to talk of treating triumph and disaster as impostors. Be prepared, I tell myself. The words have a familiar ring. They are the scout motto. But the dread of what will happen tomorrow is deadweight on my nerves, and I don't know if my scouting skills can lift it.

70

TUESDAY

When on Tuesday morning I wake to my imprisonment, I again feel dread, but I console myself that today, at the very least, there will be some kind of movement. And indeed, after a breakfast of porridge, armed guards take us to court.

Somebody from Kahũgũinĩ recognizes me: John, a teacher, but not at Kahũgũinĩ proper. He taught with Lady Teacher, in the same school. We last met on the day of my Fall from Grace, not so long ago. He walks toward me, asking loudly, *Mwalimu*, what is the matter, but he is not allowed to shake hands with me. Quickly I tell him that I have been in this situation since Friday. He has come to sort out matters with the education office. He will come to the court as soon as he is through.

The courtroom is full. I feel weak in body but happy at seeing my brothers and sisters, Kenneth, and a few other people from Limuru. I still don't know what I will be charged with, but I assume that it will have something to do with taxes. I have never been inside a courtroom before. Very quickly the accused are called out, one by one. Most of those held for taxes plead guilty. They are fined and leave the room to pay for their freedom. Other minor offenses are dealt with in a similar fashion: charge, guilty plea, fine, freedom. I am surprised at their pleas because throughout our days and nights together they all stressed their innocence. The court adjourns for a ten o'clock break. My name has not been called. The others tell me they pleaded guilty simply to avoid another night in jail. One or two don't have the money, and they ask me for a loan. I oblige where I can without depleting myself.

71

I don't know how, but during the break, while still guarded, Messrs. Rifleman and Machine Gun approach me. They are incredibly friendly, even sympathetic. They offer advice. All my friends, as they call my fellow inmates, had pleaded guilty. They were released after paying only a slight fine. I have a choice: accept guilt and be free, or refuse and face a prolonged trial and almost certainly a term in prison, which would ruin my college plans. Their advice, completely disinterested, is that I should opt for freedom. I am young, I have dreams to pursue. The police are going to help me. If I say yes, they will give testimony about my good behavior. That will be the end of my tribulations. The judges might even set me free without a fine. But if I don't cooperate, I should not blame them for whatever befalls me.

It is impossible to believe that people who have been so cruel to me could now be so completely sympathetic, so ready to help me achieve my freedom. They have presented themselves as if they were the only genuine friends I have in the world. I don't say anything, not wanting to argue. I am completely isolated from the company of family and friends whom I see around, which deepens my loneliness. The nightmare I used to have in my early days at Alliance about bloodhounds at the gate comes back in a different form: they still pursue me, but when I shout for help, people don't hear me, passing by without a glance in my direction.

The court resumes. It is full again. Even those already discharged have come back to hear my case. I am in the dock, alone, guarded. Everything is a first time for me. Messrs. Rifleman and Machine Gun, my recently self-avowed friends, are in the courtroom. There is a glint of evil in the eyes of the lead officer, Mr. Rifleman, reminding me that if I don't accept guilt, I should be ready to face the consequences. I am still expecting to be charged with not paying taxes. I begin to wonder if I should follow in the footsteps of the others. It is not a matter of law and justice; it is a choice between prison and college.

But when the charge is read, I am flabbergasted. I cannot believe my ears: there is absolutely no mention of taxes. Instead I am charged with resisting arrest and assaulting a police officer on duty. There is a gasp in the audience: they all know that under the state of emergency, it would be suicidal to resist arrest, let alone actually assault a police officer. I am asked to enter a plea, but instead I stand up and try to explain my innocence. No, all I am needed to say is yes or no to the charge. I want to explain, to tell the truth of what happened, but the presiding judge is saying no, no, just say yes or no, you'll have a chance to explain later. I am on the verge of tears. I see conspiracy all around me. Why won't they let me explain that the charge itself is a pack of lies? They can see that I am completely innocent of court procedures. In the end, they write down that I have pleaded not guilty. I sit down. The trial begins.

The judge-chairman asks if the prosecutor is ready to proceed with the witnesses. Yes, he says, consulting Mr.

Rifleman, who goes out, followed quickly by Mr. Machine Gun. Mr. Rifleman comes back fairly quickly and whispers something. The prosecutor apologizes to the court. His key witness has just been called on urgent duty and will not be available that day. I don't need an expert to tell me that this will mean postponing proceedings and my return to the remand prison for an undefined length of time. The council of judges confers. Then the verdict: the officer must produce his witnesses the following morning when the court resumes.

72

They take me back to the remand prison. It is all a conspiracy. How could the presiding council of elders give any credence to barefaced lies? Even now I am not allowed to confer with my relatives and friends. My worsted woolen trousers have still not lost their creases, but I know that they must be stinking.

In the prison yard, Mr. Rifleman and Mr. Machine Gun, the officer supposedly called on duty, come back to me. They pull me aside. Were these not the witnesses said to be unavailable? I ask myself bitterly. They return to the same story and the same theme: surrender to save yourself. The charge is very serious; it will mean a long prison term, and I may as well say goodbye to my dreams of college. When the court resumes tomorrow, I should ask to change my plea: the police will vouch for my behavior. Their demeanor, tone, gesture, everything, exudes sympathy and a genuine desire to help. They explain that they did not produce the witnesses because they wanted to give me more time to consider. So even the lie to the judge was to help me? I don't say anything. But when they leave, I feel completely abandoned.

The old inmates have all gone, even Mr. Bank Robber and Mr. Body Parts. All the friends I knew have been replaced by a new lot of frightened inmates. But the stories, the walls, the toilets, the stink, and the blankets are all familiar. There are lice in my hair, but even the incessant itching cannot distract me from my sense of isolation.

Throughout the night, shadows of doubt visit me. Suppose Mr. Rifleman is right? Suppose . . . suppose this and that . . . the future becomes bleaker by the minute. The sweet persuasive voice to do what is easy increases in volume. It's so easy to plead guilty, pay a fine, and then continue with life. But in pleading guilty, I would be telling a lie, ensuring that their lies become a permanent truth about me. I am still wrestling with doubts and indecision as dawn comes and they take me back to the courtroom.

73

WEDNESDAY

Word has spread; the court is even more packed than yesterday. At the door, John, the teacher from Kahũgũinĩ, hands me an envelope, then disappears among the crowd.

I put it in my pocket. The Limurian faces of yesterday have returned, and more. John of the Envelope must have spread the word.

Eventually, the judges enter. They ask if the prosecutor has his witnesses. The officers are still in the field, he tells the court. It will take a couple of days to produce them. He is asking for another postponement, ready to proceed with other cases, equally pressing. Again there's an adjournment for them to consider his request. The wheels of justice are slow. I am still under armed guard, still isolated from relatives and friends I can see but cannot touch.

Suddenly I remember the envelope. Something to distract my mind. I open it. *I had lived with doubts. You answered my doubts. You helped me see the Lord. Jesus will help you. Say a prayer. I'm doing the same for you. Signed Lady Teacher, your Sister in Christ.* Is it a hoax, a joke, a mockery? Then the irony, or the absurdity, dawns on me. In all my Balokole days, inside and outside Alliance, I had failed to convert a single soul. Now this note is telling me that in my fall I have succeeded. Was it because I had been addressing my own doubts, and my voice carried sincerity and conviction? I close my eyes and pray. I still don't hear any voice speaking back to me.

How could Carey Francis have lived a life of such complete acceptance and obedience to an invisible master? How does he know whether he is obeying the commands of a higher being? How does he believe? Doubt has always pursued me, even during the height of our three-person cabal. For there are things I cannot believe in, no matter how hard I try to convince myself: virgin births; God literally born as an ordinary human child; physical resurrection and ascension to Heaven. Gaitho and his marriage of history and eschatology make more sense to me than all the revival meetings I attended. Except now I am thinking of survival not revival. But what if revival guarantees survival? *God works in mysterious ways his wonders to perform.* I murmur a prayer for the strength to do what I have to do, and for forgiveness in advance of my doing it. Is it an illusion, or do I hear a voice saying, yes, heed what the police advise, they may be the instruments of God's will. They have arrested me and now have offered a clear way out, the way that has been followed by the majority of the other inmates, who have all been set free for the simple act of pleading guilty and begging for clemency from the court.

When the panel of judges comes back, they deny the prosecutor his request for another postponement. Unless they have witnesses, the court has no alternative . . . No, your honors, please wait for me to check. Whispers. A police officer goes out and comes back, followed by Mr. Rifleman. Suddenly, miraculously, one witness has materialized. If the panel is surprised, they don't show it by word or gesture. Mr. Rifleman is sworn on the Bible to tell the truth, the whole truth, and nothing but the truth. But the moment he opens his mouth, he spews lie after lie. He puts on a flawless performance. He even puts on an air of humility: it pains him to have to testify about these awful deeds against a youth with so much promise. But law is law, and as a police officer, he must uphold it. Your honor, this youth thinks he is above the law, just because he has been to Alliance High School and was taught by Carey Francis.

His narrative is seamless. He obviously assumes that lies smoothly delivered can smother truth. At Alliance, though not said in so many words, there was an assumption that we should always give credence, or the benefit of the doubt, to authority. At home my mother was always adamant that we not call an adult a liar to his face. But how does one give the benefit of the doubt to fiction dressed as fact? Or not call out an adult who lies brazenly?

A lunch break. The court is back in the afternoon. It is now my turn. Surrender. End it all. One word, yes, and it is all over. God's will. Freedom bought with a lie. Why not? Betrayal brought about Christian salvation, I remind myself. The court clerk reads the charge to me. I hesitate. Then I recall the words my mother sent through my brother Wallace on day one of my incarceration: *Truth never dies.* It directly translates as truth never lies. She is not in the court-room, but I see the pain on her face, feel it in her voice: is that the best you can do? *Ũguo no guo wona ũngĩhota?* They repeat the charge. I am trembling. But when finally I find my voice, it is loud and clear: I am not guilty.

74

With those words, I have fought back. The relief I feel is tremendous. I am at peace, not thinking about the consequences anymore. I simply want to get my side of the story out. I try to trace it back to when I got my salary with arrears and how I was anxious to get home to my mother. They stop me and tell me to ask Mr. Rifleman questions. The conspiracy again. Why should I ask him questions instead of telling my story? It is hopeless. I don't know what to say, what to ask.

And then, out of nowhere, I recall my days with the Alliance debating society, the parliamentary format, in which you asked questions and, in the process, brought out inconsistencies in the opponent's position. I decide that Mr. Rifleman is the mover of the government motion, and I am the opposition. I am back in my Alliance element. Do you remember that I was on the bus from Nairobi to Limuru? Yes. Do you remember that you entered the bus? Yes. And that you had a gun, a rifle, and your partner, a machine gun? He hesitates. The elders ask him to answer: Were you armed? Yes. What weapon? A rifle. And your partner? A machine gun. Continue with your questions. And you remember I was not armed, in any way? Well, but you had a parcel. What kind of parcel? The court forces him to admit that a parcel is not a weapon. Question after question, I go through the entire story, how he asked me for tax papers, and what I told him. Do you remember telling me that even Kiano, Mboya, and Oginga Odinga pay taxes? No. And from there onward, he responds to my every question with no, which of course makes him contradict himself over and over again. I am relentless. I feel a new power, the power of telling the truth. I can be consistent; he cannot. Through questions, my story unfolds up to and including their attempts to ask me to plead guilty. No, no, they were simply asking me to tell the truth. The court is so silent that one can hear a pin drop. When I finish, there is applause, which is met with a stern rebuke from the court.

One of the elders asks me if I have the Makerere and Alliance papers over which I claimed the police officer mocked me. I pass them to the court. The court adjourns. But people do not leave the room for fear of losing their seats.

I am still under guard. The way people look at me in the room makes me feel that something I don't quite understand has happened. I am not relaxed. I still smart at the fact that I was not allowed to tell my narrative in my own way. But I feel good that I did not succumb to the temptation to say yes to a lie.

By the time the court resumes, a crowd of those not able to get inside has gathered all around the building. The hour of judgment has come. It is simple: the court will not stand in the way of a young man who has just graduated from Alliance with such grades. Police officers must not let jealousy cloud their judgment in the execution of their duties. This court will not stand between you and Makerere, the judge says. You are free to go.

For a few seconds, I am not able to take it in. I feel tears, and I don't know if they are of joy or horror at how closely I came to damning my soul forever by lying out of fear. The audience is restrained. Everybody leaves the courtroom except for Messrs. Rifleman and Machine Gun. Even their fellow officers seem to have abandoned them. Outside, people are talking animatedly, laughing, cheering.

The crowd from Kahũgũinĩ. The crowd from Kamĩrĩthũ. I don't feel a stranger to my village anymore. It has taken a long time. But the gain of the new makes up for the loss of the old. Good Wallace embraces me. My younger brother, Njinju, clings to my hand, making it clear to all that I am his hero. I feel overwhelmed with relief. I will not let this ordeal mar my memories of my four-year sojourn in the House of the Interpreter or my expectations of the future.

Little did I know that this ordeal would turn out to be a rehearsal for others ahead. That's another story, another place, another time. Nothing will ever dim the glory of the hour when I became free, or diminish my longing and quest for freedom, whose value I have come to cherish even more.

75

In July 1959 I was back in Limuru railway station, boarding a passenger train bound for Kampala, Uganda. In the second-class section, no longer reserved for Asians only, were many Alliance graduates, old and new, going to Makerere University College. As the train picked up speed, the children's song we used to attribute to the Kampala train played in my mind: *Ndathiĩ, Uganda*. To-U-Ganda, To-U-Ganda, To-U-Ganda.

Acknowledgments

I would like to thank all who helped me recover this memory, particularly: my wife, Njeeri wa Ngũgĩ, for commenting on the various versions of the story; the principal of Alliance, Mr. D. G. Kariuki, and the head of English at Alliance, Mr. M. Muchiri, for receiving me at the school and providing me with the Carey Francis log, a precious mine of information on dates and events; Joe Kihara Munugu, Gatua wa Mbũgua, Eliud Kihara, Allan Ngũgĩ, Kimani Nyoike, Archibald Githinji, Philip Ochieng, Kĩmunya Ngũgĩ, Kenneth King, Gordon C. Mwangi, Albert Kariuki Ng'ang'a, Kamau Kĩariĩ, and Emilia Ilieva, for their help in collecting material for this memoir; Mũkoma wa Ngũgĩ, Mũmbi W. Ngũgĩ, Thiongo K. Ngũgĩ, and Bjorn Lanno for debating various titles; and Barbara Caldwell for research. Gloria Loomis and Henry Chakava read the initial drafts and made useful suggestions; Erroll McDonald edited it with care and respect for the spirit. Bits and pieces of the memoir have been published in the following magazines: *10TAL, Istanbul Review, Über Lebenskunst, Index on Censorship.* The first public reading of selections from the memoir was at the annual end-and-beginning-of-the-year performance festival at Professor Gaby Schwab's house in University Hills at the University of California, Irvine.

Printed in the United States
by Baker & Taylor Publisher Services